The Voyage to Your Vision
Top Experts Chart the Course for Your Professional
and Personal Journey to Success

The Voyage to Your Vision
Top Experts Chart the Course for Your Professional and Personal Journey to Success

©2014 by Experts Insights Publishing,
Viki Winterton

Expert Insights Publishing

1001 East WT Harris Blvd #247
Charlotte, NC 28213

All rights reserved. No part of this book may be reproduced in any manner whatsoever, and it may not be stored in a retrieval system, transmitted, or otherwise copied for public or private use, without written permission other than "fair use" as brief quotations embodied in articles and reviews.

ISBN: 978-0-9837379-9-5

Cover Design: Terry Z

Edited by: Pam Murphy, Wendy Rumrill

Interviews: Viki Winterton

15 14 13 12 11   1 2 3 4 5

A portion of the proceeds from the sale of this book will be donated to One Child Matters.

_____Dedication_____

To Anabel Pena
Dominican Republic
One Child Matters
Sponsored by the Authors of this Book
who support you on the Voyage to Your Vision!

Table of Contents

Introduction
I. Voyage to Success — 9

Ch. 1 Make Your Dreams Come True, Marcia Wieder — 10
Ch. 2 Become a Fearless Leader, Dr. Cathy L. Greenberg — 18
Ch. 3 Make Media Magic, Rick Frishman — 26
Ch. 4 Become an Instant Celebrity, Clint Arthur — 36
Ch. 5 Find Your Authentic Success, Shari Yantes — 50
Ch. 6 Ask "Why Not" Instead Of "Why," Gary Barnes — 58
Ch. 7 Power Your Dreams, Dorothy Kuhn — 66
Ch. 8 Get the Key Concepts to Success, Chaffee-Thanh Nguyen — 78
Ch. 9 Learn Before You Launch, Barbara Bamba — 86
Ch. 10 Discover Your Passion, Donald Gilbert, Ph.D. — 96
Ch. 11 Change Your Brain for Success, Dr. Simone Ravicz — 102
Ch. 12 Build Your Wealth, Paul Lawrence Vann — 108
Ch. 13 Be Excellent, Luis Vicente Garcia — 116
Ch. 14 Express Yourself, Viki Winterton — 126
Ch. 15 Discover Your "Why," Divya Parekh — 132
Ch. 16 From Problems to Possibilities, Dr. Richard Eley — 146
Ch. 17 Achieve Through Education, Elizabeth Olagunju — 156

II. Voyage to Relationships — 165

Ch. 18 Make One Child Matter, Mike Fritz — 166
Ch. 19 Claiming Your Heroic Heart, Hal Price — 176

Ch. 20 Act On Love™, Dr. Mamiko Odegard	186

III. Voyage to Wellness — 197
Ch. 21 Heal Through Humor, Allen Klein — 198
Ch. 22 Crisis Response, Denise Joy Thompson — 206
Ch. 23 Realize Your True Value, Dr. Francesca A. Jackson — 214
Ch. 24 Awaken, Geri Portnoy — 222
Ch. 25 Develop Your Humanity, Anne Redelfs, MD — 232

IV. Voyage to Spirituality and Fulfillment — 243
Ch. 26 Follow Your Transformational Path, Louise Finlayson — 244
Ch. 27 No Excuses, Drew Hunthausen — 252
Ch. 28 Unite for Success, Sabrina Williams — 266
Ch. 29 Make a Difference, Lauren Perotti — 272
Ch. 30 You Too Can Do, Susanne Whited — 280
Ch. 31 Your Rites of Passage, Rev. M. Azima Jackson, MS, DMin — 288
Ch. 32 Sneak Peek to Possibilities, Dr. Tianna Conte, ND — 296
Ch. 33 HOPE, Carol Davies — 312

Words of Wisdom and Vision — 317
Complimentary Resources — 329
Index — 336
About Expert Insights Publishing — 339

Introduction

All of us have the capacity to become what we want to be and achieve what we want to contribute to the world. After all, each one of us is blessed with the unique skills and abilities that are needed to become successful. It's up to us which of these talents we will develop and use. However, on the path to success, we will undergo a wonderful and adventurous voyage.

The Vision

"The first step is always the hardest." This is also true when it comes to the path of success. If we want to become successful, we have to know which path we choose to take. When we, as individuals continuously developing, our interests continue to change and grow as well. Making the decision as to what we want our life to look like personally and professionally is not an easy task, as it requires the balance of our abilities, skills and our passion. However, if we are clear in our choice, our minds and actions will be gracefully guided on the path to reach our goals.

The Voyage

We all have our unique journeys. We need to be willing to face any challenge if we have really set our heart and mind on living our passion and purpose. Being successful is not just about reaching the goal; it can also be measured on what we are willing to do in order to see our mission fulfilled.

The Value of Lessons Learned

As we experience challenges, we become stronger. Hence, in any kind of hardship, there is a fabulous lesson we can learn. As we each go along our personal adventure — a voyage often filled with trials, every situation offers us something important and necessary to continue our journey. And these experiences are important in teaching us new behavior and providing us new tools that are beneficial both professionally and in real-life personal situations.

Words of Wisdom and Vision

The voyage to our vision makes us wiser. It helps us form our values and principles. When we are willing to share these experiences as tips and suggestions to others, they can become invaluable, change lives and help others define and achieve their success.

Voyage to Success

1. Make Your Dreams Come True
Marcia Wieder

Dream University's® CEO/Founder **Marcia Wieder** is committed to helping one million dreams come true over the next year.

The author of 14 books, she has appeared on *Oprah* and *The TODAY Show* and has been featured on her own PBS TV show called "Making Your Dreams Come True." As a columnist for the *San Francisco Chronicle*, her column urged readers to take "The Great Dream Challenge."

Marcia is a member of the Transformational Leadership Council with Jack Canfield and John Gray.

As a past president of the National Association of Women Business Owners, she has assisted three U.S. presidents. She also serves on the advisory board for the Make-A-Wish Foundation. dreamuniversity.com

My Vision

I am committed to helping one million dreams come true over the next year! A dream is simply something that you want; it is made up. Some dreams are based on need and some of them are based on desire, but the dreams that are the expression of your purpose and your mission are usually the most profound. We could say that standing in your purpose is where the quality of your dreams and the quality of your life will change.

The difference between a dream and a fantasy—like winning the lottery—is that in a dream, you can actually design a strategy for getting there. On the other hand, there is nothing you can do to ensure that you win the lottery. If you never strategize regarding your dream, it remains simply a fantasy or a nice idea.

If you begin strategic thinking too early in the process, that will often cause you to compromise your dream down to only what you realistically believe is possible. However, if you never get into strategy and action, the dream just remains a fantasy. It's like you have to hang out just long enough in the dreaming phase before you get into strategy and action.

For me, a goal is what you discover once you become clear about your dream. At a certain point, you have to assign due dates and get very specific, but not right out of the gate. The idea behind dreaming is to get you to swing outside of just being realistic and to ask yourself questions like, "If time and money weren't issues, you had the support of the people around you, and you knew you could not fail, what would you do?" That's what opens up the dreaming conversation.

You have to know where you are in order to design the strategy for where you want to go. The real question to ask yourself is, "What has being realistic cost you?" If you're overly realistic, not only can that cost you your passion and your dreams, but Dr. Mehmet Oz personally taught me that people with passion and dreams actually live seven to ten years longer; being overly realistic can literally cost you years of your life.

There's a funny word called "apoptosis." Apoptosis—just like it sounds—refers to when your brain believes you've outgrown your usefulness. This can happen at any age, but we see it most often when people retire, get laid off, experience an empty nest, or stop dreaming. The brain sends a message to the body that it's no longer needed, and people start to mentally or physically self-destruct.

My Voyage

I would say that one of my personal goals is to change the way we think about and speak about our dreams. So instead of telling yourself, "Maybe someday" or "When I have the time and money" or "When the kids graduate" or "When I retire," it's really about getting clear about what you want, believing in yourself, and proving your belief by taking action. That's where the rubber meets the road and it gets very real.

Purpose and mission are the foundation. It's best conveyed through that old adage: "If you climb to the top of the mountain without knowing your purpose or your mission, you may only find out that sometimes it's the wrong mountain." We see that and hear that a lot. As I said earlier, by standing in your purpose, the quality of your dreams and the quality of your life will change. For me, purpose answers the question,

"Who am I?" Then my dreams answer, "How do I want my life to be?"

The Value of Lessons Learned

I think living with purpose requires three elements:

1. A spiritual practice so that you can get quiet, still, and hear the deeper wisdom underneath the ego.

2. Knowledge of what's unique and special about you.

3. A way to be of service using that characteristic.

The people who live with purpose are usually the people who are the most fulfilled. We spend most of our time with people who don't know their purpose at the Dream Coach Certification program and even at the one-day Create Your Future Now program. We are able to help people identify what their purpose is, and it's a game-changer.

As coaches, we know that knowing our own purpose and helping others find theirs is incredibly satisfying. It really can change everything once people really know who they are. We're in the small percentage of people in the world who actually have the luxury to ask the question, "What is my purpose?" I think the people who can answer that question have a *responsibility* to ask that question.

Once you ask the questions, "Who am I and how do I want my life to be?" if you're somebody who practices living with integrity, the next question must be, "What am I willing to do about it?" Having the courage to say, "No more" or "No thank you" to what's no longer true or necessary and scheduling more things in your life that truly are an expression of the purpose of your mission—your heart and soul—that's what living a dream-come-true life is really all about.

In my Dream Coach Program, instead of the ABCs, we have these CBAs:

C: Get **clear** about what you want. For most people, that's the hardest step. It involves writing it down and talking about it and getting it out of your head.

B: Believe in yourself and your dreams—this is a choice. Can you believe in something simply because it matters to you, and not because there are promises, guarantees, or assurances?

A: Act on your dreams to prove that you really do believe in them. Get clear about your dreams, believe in your dreams, and act on your dreams.

Dreams; these actions are, in a nutshell, at the simplest level of what my program's about.

Step one is an intention, which is the rudder that steers the course of your life.

Step two is living with integrity. Intention and integrity together form the core building blocks for manifestation. You can't have one without the other. The ultimate form of integrity is not just keeping your agreements with others or yourself, but also keeping your agreements with God at a spiritual level. That takes us to Step three, which is about **living on purpose**, which we just talked about.

Intention, Integrity, Purpose, and Access your dreamer.

There seems to be a sacred relationship between those last

two. If you turn the voice of the doubter down, you hear the voice of the realist who pretty much wants to know, "What's the plan?" Mostly it wants to know where you are going to get the time and the money. Before you turn it down, you might want to hear from it, because the doubter will give you your list of obstacles. All obstacles either require an existing belief, a new belief, or a strategy to manage them.

Step three is living on purpose.

Step four is accessing your dreamer.

Step five is believing in your dreams.

Step six is establishing personal practices. You need to really focus in on whatever your Achilles' heel is and develop a practice to strengthen or change it.

Step seven is creating projects and strategies. People are always saying, "Wait a minute, you don't get to strategy and projects until Step seven?" Well, it's not really a linear process. At any point, you might want to go back and revisit your intention or your integrity, your doubts or your beliefs, but as I said when I first began, people tend to go to strategy too quickly, so it's better to reach this later, after you've really opened yourself up to the dream and your belief in yourself and your dream, because that opens you up to much more possibility.

Step eight is building your dream team, which has to do with mastering enrollment. If you master manifestation, then you've mastered the skill of enrollment. That refers to your ability to share your dream in a way that inspires other people to join you, to hire you, and to invest in you. You do that by making specific requests and making it easy for people to say "yes" to you.

Finally, **Step nine** is living as a dreamer and realizing that this entire process can be used on any dream—a personal or professional relationship, your health, your community, or your financial and spiritual goals! Ultimately, once you really develop skills and cultivate who you are as a dreamer, it means you get an idea and act on it, and then you really get to live your dream-come-true life.

I've met amazing dreamers like Oprah, but it's really the everyday people and the phenomenal coaches of the world who I think are really leading this dream movement. I have coached Jack Canfield. I've been training a thousand coaches. As coaches, we are visionaries, and we have to believe in our clients' dreams as well as our own.

Share your dream with others—and it's how you share it that makes a difference. If you think about it, a visionary has big dreams, articulates them with clarity so people understand them, expresses them with passion so people are excited about them, and then invites other people to join them.

If you can do what you love, value who you are, charge what you're worth, have powerful conversations, and repeat these steps often, most likely you'll be very successful in sharing your gifts with the world at a time when the world really needs your gifts.

Don't look at your life and say, "Well, my life doesn't look like that purpose." Instead, make the choices and changes in your life so you align your life with who you are, not vice versa. I think that, when you're really open to knowing who you are and what your life is in service of, it shows up.

Oprah Winfrey said that her dream was to create a company in which people would come together, make a contribution, and give back to the world together. The audience went crazy. During the commercial break, Oprah came over to me and she said, "Marcia, you know something that I know. It's all about believing in your dreams."

Oprah stated if she had to attribute her success in life to any one thing, it was that she believed in her dreams, even when no one else did.

What I'll add to Oprah's wisdom is that sometimes there's no evidence that your dream is a good idea or that this is the right time to pursue it, but the question is this: "Where are you looking for evidence?" Don't look for evidence of whether or not you should believe in your dream in your checkbook, in the stock market, or on the news—those are terrible places to look.

Words of Wisdom and Vision

The place to look to decide whether or not you believe in your dreams is in your own heart. Ask yourself this: Can you believe in something simply because it matters to you and then demonstrate that you really do believe in it by taking action? Then, and only then, does it actually have a real chance of survival in your life.

2. Become a Fearless Leader
Dr. Cathy L. Greenberg

Dr. Cathy L. Greenberg is a professional certified coach. She leads executives and entire companies on her Happiness = Profits strategy. She's been named the First Lady of Happiness by ABC-TV.

Dr. Greenberg has multiple popular books on the science of happiness including *What Happy Companies Know* and *What Happy Working Mothers Know*.

She touches millions as a much in demand speaker, TV, radio, and media personality. Cathy also has a brand new book and program series, *Fearless Leaders*, with more tips and tools. DrCathyGreenberg.com.

My Vision

I actually was a partner at two of the world's largest consulting firms. One was Computer Sciences Corporation. Then I went to a company at the time known as Anderson Consulting. They evolved into the company, Accenture, where I eventually retired from when we IPO'd. While I was a graduate student and prior to deciding what I wanted to do with my life, a career in consulting (which is where I am now), I had studied sociobiology – an interesting little subject – which is the study of the science and biology of humankind. It was something that I had never anticipated being a foundation for the work that I do now in emotional and social intelligence and the science of happiness, and now the new science of fearlessness and the science of courage.

I have had wonderful mentors. Warren Bennis, who is the father of leadership, Noel Tichy, Jim Kouzes – many, many wonderful people have over the years inspired me, adopted me, and helped me integrate their thinking into what we now know as the science of leadership. Many of us didn't realize that back in the 1960s and 1970s, and even into the 1980s. People could not measure leadership in a hard way. We called it the "soft science" but we now know that these things are measurable; they are quantifiable. As a person who likes to think of themselves as a bit of a psychometrician, I appreciate the fact, along with emotional intelligence and the science of happiness, that we now have national and global entities, foundations, that do nothing but measure leadership, management, emotional intelligence; and as we now know, we call it the positive psychology of the human condition and optimism.

My Voyage

It's never easy, and I think everyone who is reading this has a point in time in life when we realize that the journey we're on has off-ramps and on-ramps. I had a young daughter. I had been going through a divorce. Both of my parents had recently passed. I was – how shall I say this – not in touch with myself. I was not mindful of what was happening to me. I was running myself into the ground as an executive in one of the world's largest consulting firms at the time, Accenture. I was managing over 1,000 people on three continents and working with over 260,000 employees worldwide. The statistics probably changed monthly on that.

The bottom line was, I was overdoing it. As my friend Marshall Goldsmith would say, I was adding too much value to the world at a cost to myself. Often we do that. We do that as executives, we do that as parents, we do that as people in loving relationships. There are those of us in the world who are givers. Sometimes when we give too much of ourselves, we get out of balance and our immune systems, unfortunately, are the targets of that wrongdoing on our behalf.

It wasn't until I went down in a plane on my way to a meeting ... I went down in a plane literally in Atlanta, Georgia. I wound up in Emory University Hospital, where I was told then that I had two potentially life-threatening illnesses, and that woke me up. I was on my way to work, and that woke me up. It was like, "Okay, we have to get our life in gear here."

I have learned about the science of happiness, the science of courage and fearlessness, and spent many, many years working with wonderful people in our industry on emotional intelligence including my cohost on our radio show, "Leadership Development News," Relly Nadler, my wonderful global leadership partner at Accenture, Alastair Robertson, and many people like Daniel Goleman and others. I've learned that when we are emotionally intelligent in happiness and optimism and how we apply that in our lives, we can make changes by choice. By choice, I was able to make changes.

By choice, I was able to consciously be mindful about what was right for me and those I was working with and for, and partnering in the global workplace to help them succeed.

I started making the right choices.

As a result, I got back on track, and everything I learned I've written about in several books. I've written several books with Marshall Goldsmith, but the one that has been his continuing launching point for almost all of his books including *MOJO* and *What Got You Here Won't Get You There,* and his newest book coming out called *Triggers,* comes from our work at Accenture, still the largest leadership development effort related to future leaders that we know of in the research to date. It's been a pleasure being able to take everything I've learned and now give it back in my new book called *Fearless Leader: Sharpen Your Focus* co-authored with TC North.

The Value of Lessons Learned

I've learned a lot from my friends like Marshall Goldsmith and Ken Blanchard over the years, and through universities where I have been affiliated – Drexel University, and I am now participating in a think tank with some executives at LaSalle. I'm a member of an organization, which is unbelievable, called The Honor Foundation. This is an institute whose mission is to transition our special operations working warriors from their current status in Navy Special Warfare and other special operations groups into civilian careers.

I'm so proud to be affiliated with these institutes. The Honor Foundation is at the Rady School of Management at UCSD, which is one of the top, if not the number one business school in Southern California.

One of the things I've learned from these wonderful affiliations is that when you include others in your work and your writing, when you reach out to others while you're writing for research, for their insights, they're so quick to support and assist, and they'll send you their research. You will be surprised how easy it is to extend yourself to include others in your work.

If I may say something without annoying anyone who's reading this and any academic who has ever published anything without referencing others, I find it so silly and so self-serving to believe that every thought that an individual has is simply de novo. It's as though sometimes people think they're the first to ever have that thought; and while I think it's outstanding if they do, I always assume that I have not.

I make the assumption I could not be the first person to see this. I could not be the first person to recognize this, nor should I be elitist enough to think that I'm the first person to write about it.

What I try to do is validate myself. Validate my ideas. Validate my thinking. Go out and find the references that do so. Then, when I reach out to those people and I say, "I've been looking at this issue and I've kind of evolved this thought into a, b, and c …

what do you think?" then you have them endorsing your thinking.

Now that's the secret sauce, because when you mention those people and their contributions to your evolving ideas, you've got an instant audience. You're being authentic, you're being real, and you're being practical about your thinking, your ideas, and where the evolution of that concept came from, and where it's going.

What I learned as a graduate student is when you make a bid for a piece of information and you put that bid out to a number of experts in the industry and they get back to you with what their thinking is on that bid for information, you're starting to not only qualify yourself as an "expert" seeking insight from experts, but you now begin to qualify yourself as an individual who is integrative, who is respectful of the mindset and the history that has come before you.

Merely by doing that with that simple bid of an email, the extension of a letter, or attending a conference and walking up to someone afterwards, giving them your paper, something you've published, something of interest to them, something that would support their ideas, you create a bid for a relationship.

It's a very simple formula, making this bid and contributing. I think a very wise man once said, "If you want something in life, you must give something in return."

It's such a powerful motto that I do live by. I've learned it many, many times over from many wonderful people.

Words of Wisdom and Vision

As I mentioned earlier, it's been a pleasure being able to take everything I've learned and now give it back in our new book called *Fearless Leader: Sharpen Your Focus,* co-authored with TC North. In my new book, we tell the world the success secrets of Olympic athletes, sports athletes, professionals, executives, humanitarians, and special operations forces that we have learned in our 30+ year careers individually that we have collectively contributed to this book.

It was just reviewed by the Pentagon. It was an informal review. We will gladly have endorsements from sports celebrities, business celebrities, generals, ambassadors, heads of state, and of course, individuals in our industry – professional coaches – who are incredibly inspired by the four principles in this book. They are:

    Act with inspiring courage.

    Respond with resilience.

    Think from a higher consciousness.

    Engage with a mindset for success.

We call that the "Art of Fearless Leading." The book is filled with wonderful stories and examples of fearless leaders throughout history. We're not only fortunate but incredibly honored to be able to include in this book stories of our own special operators who have been highlighted in wonderful movies like *The Act of Valor*, *Zero Dark Thirty*, *Captain Phillips*, and I could go on. I think the kinds of individuals that we have included in this book are just unbelievable.

3. Make Media Magic
Rick Frishman

Rick Frishman is the founder of Planned Television Arts and has been one of the leading book publicists in America for more than 30 years. Rick has worked with many top book editors, literary agents, and publishers in America and with best-selling authors including Mitch Albom, Bill Moyers, Stephen King, Caroline Kennedy, Howard Stern, and President Jimmy Carter.

Rick is the publisher at Morgan James Publishing in New York. Rick has appeared on hundreds of radio shows and more than a dozen TV shows nationwide, including *Oprah* and Bloomberg TV. He has also been featured in the *New York Times, Wall Street Journal, Associated Press, Selling Power Magazine, New York Post*, and scores of other publications. He is the co-author of 11 books, including national best-sellers *Guerilla Publicity, Networking Magic*, and *Guerrilla Marketing for Writers*. RickFrishman.com

My Vision

I always wanted to be an author. I've worked with every major publisher in the country. I've worked with about 100 literary agents. My problem is that I am a terrible writer.

I've sold a couple hundred thousand books, and I don't even know how to write. I'd like to share about how to get a lot of publicity for little or no money, and why everyone should become an author. It's fun! It will catapult your career and the media will seek you out because you're an author. If you want to become an author, the chances are that you're going to be one because we can help you.

My Voyage

I'm just an old PR guy. I started as a radio producer in New York, producing for a guy who is still on the air now, named Barry Farber. The building is actually right down the block from where I am today at WOR radio.

It was a great honor being a guest on his show almost 30 years after I produced it. I was a TV/Radio Major at Ithaca College and graduated in 1976. I joined a company called Planned TV Arts when I finished producing. My host actually ran for mayor. You can't have a radio show if you're running for public office so he lost his show, and I joined a gentleman named Mike Levine. It was just the two of us.

We built it up to be the biggest book PR company in America. At one point, I had about 60 people making more than 1,000 calls every day to producers, editors, and booking authors. I've worked with a lot of famous and infamous people.

Some were unknown authors when we first started, and now they are very well known, and some of them very rich, too.

I started booking all of these crazy authors on radio and TV. One of the first people we booked was a guy named Wayne Dyer, and he couldn't get his book published. He self-published and sold it out of the trunk of his car. We all know Wayne Dyer today, but that was in the '70s. There were lots of authors whose careers went crazy because they were authors.

In 2000, my first book came out. I had been doing publicity for about 25 years, but no one in the media really cared. When my first book, *Guerrilla Marketing for Writers*, came out, all of a sudden the media wanted to talk to me. I was doing radio and TV shows, and thinking, "This is interesting. People care now that I'm an author," even though I didn't even write most of the book—my co-authors did.

One of the key things is finding great co-authors who know how to write. I started putting on events and bringing in publishers, editors, and agents. Even after working in the publishing business for so long, I hadn't realized I knew so much about publishing.

The Value of Lessons Learned

Understand that the media doesn't give two hoots about you; they don't care about your book; they don't care about your product; they don't care about your website. They only care if you're going to be a great guest or give them an interesting news story. They also have a very short attention span. They're very much like me. I have ADD, so I think in very short bites, and I go all over the place. It's the same with them. They only look at the bullet points. Don't ever send them a paragraph, because they're not going to read it, and don't ever call them and talk to them for more than 30 seconds, because that's all the time you have to pitch to them.

Words of Wisdom and Vision

First, let's talk about publicity. I wrote a book called, *Guerrilla Publicity.*

What we want to do is get hundreds of thousands of dollars of publicity for little or no money, become a guest on a radio show, and have an editor fall in love with you and assign a reporter to write a story about you.

With advertising, you pay for it. With publicity, you pray for it. Anybody can take out an ad in The New York Times. Pay $50,000 and you can have a full-page ad; in some sections or on some days, it can be $80,000. You could buy a one-minute ad on KABC radio in Los Angeles, or KGO radio in San Francisco or WOR where I used to work in New York, and it could cost you $1,000 a minute.

Anybody can buy time, but we want to be on as a guest, because we have credibility and because we are reacting to what's in the news. A guest spot on air or a story about you in the newspaper is worth 10 times—even 100 times—more because you are newsworthy and credible. We want to try to understand how the media works and give them what they want.

So, how are you going to get on? Through publicity. Publicity can make you as rich and famous as you want to be. So how do you get publicity?

Putting Together a Press Kit

When going after publicity, you must have a press kit. Everything in your press kit has to go on your website. PR firms will charge you $5,000 for a press kit. Here's what goes into it:

- **Press Release**: One page, with a great headline, which usually will solve a problem in some way. Explain what you do. The headline explains what you are going to teach an audience.

- **Biography**: One page, and most importantly, your USP—your Unique Selling Proposition. What makes you different from every other person? What is the main thing that makes you interesting, funny, crazy, and that will cause the media to feel like they have to have you on t h e air?

- **Suggested Questions**: The host of the show will not have read your book; they will not have read your press kit—they will get handed these questions about 10 seconds before you go on the air, and will ask you exactly what you tell them to ask you. It sounds crazy, but it's true.

- **Testimonials**: There are two types of testimonials. First, there are testimonials from clients and people who think you are a god or goddess because you've helped them. Second, there are testimonials from people who are in the media who say that you're fabulous. Also include a list of all the media you've been on. Because as a producer or editor, I want to know that you've been in *The New York Times* or *Seattle Post Intelligencer,* etc. I want to know where you've been.

Controversy Sells

We have to come up with something controversial. Watch TV—watch *Good Morning America*, *The TODAY* Show, or *The Early Show*. Also, read three newspapers a day—your local paper, *USA Today,* and *The Wall Street Journal* or *The*

New York Times. Finally, look at websites like Yahoo or any site like cnn.com before you go to sleep and see what's in the news. React to what's in the news. I don't care what it is, but take the opposite point of view.

For instance, in New York, there was a gubernatorial race. We had a well-known publicist running for governor. He put his foot in his mouth every day. He was running against Andrew Cuomo. He even basically advised parents to not let their children ever play with gay people. Every day he would say something controversial, and his ratings were like 20% and Cuomo was at 80%. He was wonderful because he said such ridiculous things that you can react to, and then you have controversy—controversy sells.

Solve the Problem

Solve a problem having to do with one of four main subjects: money, health, relationships, or sex.

Everybody cares about money. They don't have enough of it, they're spending too much, their wife spends too much, or their husband is a gambler—whatever it is. Offer a legal solution—how to send your kids to college for free, how to pick a stock broker, how to get $500 more in your pocket, or how to sell your house—anything having do with money and subjects related to money. Solve their problems.

Next is health and anything related to health. The biggest area under this subject is dieting. There are four thousand diet books that come out every January. Just about everyone in America wants to lose ten, twenty, fifty pounds by next week and doesn't know how to do it, or they do it and then they put more back on. Diabetes, health, and fitness are major topics. Just look at what infomercials are on television at two o'clock in the morning. React in order to solve the problem.

The third area is relationships. Solve a problem related to sibling rivalry, or dating—obviously a billion dollar industry, just look at the success of Match.com. Tell people how to stay married or how to get your husband to put down the toilet seat. Solve a problem related to anything having to do with relationships.

Most people think about—but don't often talk about—sex. Solve a problem in this area. Viagra and other related drugs are probably one of the biggest industries. It seems like every other commercial is a Viagra commercial. Believe me, people are thinking about it. Solve a problem having to do with relationships and sex, which go hand in hand—that's what people care about.

Solve a problem in any of those areas, and people will want you on the air. If you can do it in a fun way with a lot of passion, then they'll want to put you on.

Tips for a Great Interview

1. *Be Positive.* When we're on the air talking to people, we have to be really positive. It's very similar in an interview situation as it is when you are on TV, on the radio, or in an interview by a newspaper. You're taking a negative and saying, "Don't do that, but here are the things you *should* do."

When I talk to people about going on radio or TV for an interview, the most important thing I stress to them is what I call the "Rule of Enthusiasm." This is a rule I've had for 30 years, and we have it in our company: "If you're not fired with enthusiasm, you will be fired with enthusiasm." I wish I had made it up, but it is a quote by Vince Lombardi.

The main thing to keep in mind is that people care about your passion, your energy, and what kind of person you are, so when you're meeting them for the first time, it comes across very clearly.

Another key phrase is, "You only have one chance to make a first impression." As far as first impressions go, the biggest mistake people make is having a bad handshake. It needs to be a firm grip. Especially common for women, a limp or loose handshake is a negative thing. Have a great handshake.

2. *Make Eye Contact.* You must stay locked on their eyes. If you're uncomfortable with that for some reason, you can look at the tip of their nose.

3. *Let Them Speak.* In an interview situation or when you first meet someone, let them talk about themselves. People will think you're a wonderful conversationalist if you get them to talk about themselves. No matter what, keep asking questions. Obviously, if you're on the air, they want you to be talking as much as possible, which will make things easier on them. You will need to stop every now and then and give the host opportunities to ask questions.

4. *Be Specific.* Giving tips, lists, etc., is key, and the media love it. Lists such as "Five Mistakes Every Person Makes When Trying to Get a Job," "Seven Ways to Lose Ten Pounds by Next Week," and "Ten Secrets to Finding a Spouse Within the Next Six Months," all tap into what people are looking for—they like secrets, strategies, and the numbers five, seven, and ten.

One thing you must do when you're on the air or in an interview is to give people three specific things to do today that will change their lives. Tell them you have 45 or 126 strategies in your book or course or that you teach your clients, and then tell them you're going to share three of those right now. You're giving them specific, real, tangible things to take away.

You can also react to recent negative controversy and then turn it around and say, "Here's what you *should* be doing." Turn it into a positive thing.

I'll go one step further: Get the negative energy and negative people out of your life.

Your answers on the radio and TV should address a problem. Give an example of the problem so the particular audience or demographic—whether it's business people, CEOs, housewives, or teens—can understand. Then, offer a solution for what they can do today, and again, three specific things they can do right now. They're not going to change their whole life right away, but you give these three things to get them started down the yellow brick road.

If you give them those specifics and stay out of "esoteric land" and stay in "specific land," there's a better chance they'll say, "Yes, that's a problem I'm facing, and I didn't realize I've been doing it all wrong." They're going to want more from you and will come back for everything you can give them.

4. Become an Instant Celebrity
Clint Arthur

Clint Arthur is a graduate of the Wharton School of Business, a successful entrepreneur with over a decade of experience running his own gourmet food company, and the number one bestselling author of *The Greatest Book of All Time, The Last Year of Your Life, Daddy Loves You,* and *What They Teach You at the Wharton Business School.*

His famous personal transformation experiences, keynote speeches, and frequent appearances on network TV and syndicated radio shows inspire millions of people to live larger, more extensively, and with more impact on the world. www.instantcelebrity.com

My Vision

It all began on New Year's Eve of the millennium. Where were you? What were you doing? Were you getting Y2K money out of the ATMs?

I was pretty close by. I was driving a taxi that night in Los Angeles, California. Even though I was hanging out with hundreds of people, they were all in the backseat of my cab, and I was taking them to the parties and driving them home to their mansions. Even though I made more money that night than I would normally make in a whole week of driving a taxi, I still felt like I was the biggest loser in the world.

When I got home to my little, tiny boat that I was living on in Marina Del Ray – and don't get excited, it wasn't very glamorous; there was no running water, no electricity, no heat, no toilet facilities on the boat – I climbed into my little bunk under my heavy down comforter wearing all my heavy clothes because it was cold on the boat in the middle of winter. I pulled out my favorite book to try to read and calm down for the night with something that I loved. My favorite book was and still is *Angela's Ashes* by Frank McCourt. It is the most beautiful piece of prose in the English language. He's an Irish storyteller, and it's about his impoverished youth in Ireland. He won a Pulitzer Prize for this book.

As I was lying there reading this book probably for the tenth time, I got distracted by my breath as it was condensing in the night air in the light of my flashlight beam. I started thinking back, "How did I become a taxi driver on the most memorable New Year's Eve of everybody's life? Why me?"

You see, I was supposed to be a great writer like my creative writing teacher from high school, Frank McCourt, whose book I was reading. After I graduated from the best public high school in America, Stuyvesant High School, where Frank was my teacher for two years, I then went to the Wharton Business School – the same school as Donald Trump and all his kids. I graduated with a 4.0 GPA in my major, and I was even more inspired to make a fortune as a writer like Donald Trump, multiple *New York Times* best-selling author who made tons of money from his writing.

Then I hit a little snag. I saw a movie called *She's Got to Have It* by Spike Lee, and Spike Lee became my new idol because he wrote the movie. He created the whole thing by writing it. Then, he starred in the movie; he directed and produced the movie and made a bunch of money as an independent filmmaker. I said, "Ah-ha! That's got everything in the world that I want."

I dedicated myself to becoming the nice Jewish boy version of Spike Lee. For the next 13 years, I pursued that like nobody's business. The last six of those years, I was a taxi driver. As I lie there in my bunk, I started crying because I was terrified that I had blown all the great opportunities that I had created for myself. I was in my mid-thirties. I had no money. I had no future, other than behind the wheel of a cab. I felt like such a big loser because, at that point, I had a fraternity brother who was already a Director at Goldman Sachs making millions.

I had just traded the most memorable New Year's Eve of all time for $513 that I earned that night. I didn't know what to do. I was terrified I could never get out from behind the wheel of that cab.

I swore an oath to myself that if writing was going to put me behind the wheel of a cab, it wasn't worth it. I was going to do everything I possibly could to change who I was and how I was showing up in this world.

The first thing I did was I burned all the screenplays and all the books I had written. I'd written a bunch of books by that point, too. I tried everything as a writer. Then I started doing personal growth. I did firewalking with Tony Robbins. I did Toltec wisdom studies with Don Miguel Ruiz. I did men's power circles at ceremonies.

I did everything; and sure enough, as I began to change on the inside, the outer circumstances in my life began to change.

My Voyage

I got out of taxi driving and into the gourmet food industry. I own the Five Star Butter Company. I sell the best butter on earth to the top chefs in the world. The Waldorf Astoria in New York City is my client. The Bellagio – every piece of bread in the Bellagio is buttered with Five Star Butter.

Sure enough, I started making money. Once I started making money, I met an amazing woman. I got lucky because I met a woman who believed in me more than I ever believed in myself. She said, "Let's get involved in real estate." This was in 2002. I said, "I don't know anything about real estate, but I can learn." I bought Carlton Sheets' *No Money Down*. I bought *Rich Dad, Poor Dad*. I did self-help, learning how to do real estate.

The next thing I knew, I was in real estate. I built five houses during the great real estate boom in the early 2000s. By 2008, I was quite fat and happy. Actually, I was obese at 236 pounds,

90 pounds heavier than I was when I graduated from high school.

One night, I was at a men's self-help campfire because I stayed involved with the self-help movement of men. Lucky for me I did because that night at the campfire, the shaman pointed at me through the yellow and orange crackle and flames of the campfire and he said, "You don't know it yet, but you're already dead!"

I said, "What are you talking about, man? I was a taxi driver eight years ago, and now I'm a millionaire. I was living in a little, tiny boat, and now I'm living in a mansion. What do you mean I'm already dead?"

He said, "You're already dead. You just don't know it."

I didn't know what he was talking about, but I could not stop thinking about it. I would wake up in the middle of the night mumbling to myself, "I'm already dead. I'm already dead. What did he mean, I'm already dead?"

It came to be New Year's Day of 2009. I woke up that morning and I pulled out a pad of paper and a pen to write down my list of goals for the year. I had gotten in the habit of doing this as I became successful. Having goals is very important. I said to myself, "If this is going to be the last year of my life, what do I want to accomplish?" That question changed everything because I started living with a new energy and passion.

Surprisingly, the first thing I wrote down on the list was, "I have to write my book about what I learned at the Wharton Business School that has helped me to become successful as an entrepreneur, once I started focusing on being a successful businessman instead of trying to be a writer." I didn't expect that because I had not written a word in over eight years. The next thing I know, it's three months later, and I had a finished book.

That was awesome; the problem was, by the end of 2009, I had only sold eight copies of that book as a print on demand paperback on Amazon. I remembered what Jack Canfield told me when I met him. Having mentors, having people who you model their success, that's very, very important to being successful today. Jack Canfield said, "When we were promoting *Chicken Soup for the Soul,* we did media every single day. We committed to doing media every day."

I said, "I'm a successful businessman. I have a book about what I learned at the best business school in the world. It's a great book. I want to promote this in a big way." I called my publicist in New York and said, "Get me on the *Today* show."

She laughed at me. She said, "That's the funniest thing I've ever heard. They're never going to put you on the Today show, Clint. You're a middle-aged guy nobody's ever heard of. You have a self-published book nobody has ever bought. You have no TV experience. Why would they put you on the number one show in the world?" I said, "Well, how about NBC New York? Can I go on the morning news at NBC and tell my hometown people about what it was that raised me up from being a taxi driver to a millionaire?"

She said, "Clint, I really think I've got you figured out. You're not really a business author, you're a comedian because that's the second most hysterically funny thing you've said to me in 30 seconds! They're never going to put you on NBC New York.

You're a middle-aged guy nobody's ever heard of. You've got a self-published book nobody's ever bought, no TV experience – why would they put you on the number one station of the number one market in America? It's not going to ever happen. You have to start local."

Just then, my iPhone 3GS goes "ding!" I looked at the email that came in. It was from Southwest Airlines, and there was a route map. I said, "Okay, publicist lady, you can't do New York City – how about Salt Lake City? I could fly there cheap on Southwest Airlines."

She said, "Oh, I can do that, and it would only cost you $1,500 for me to book you on in Salt Lake City or any market outside the top 10 cities in America."

I said, "Okay, let's do it. I'll go to Salt Lake City. I'll show them how great I'm going to be, and then they'll book me right onto the *Today* show."

A couple days later, I get another "ding!" on my iPhone 3GS and lo and behold it says, "Congratulations! You're booked on television in Salt Lake City, Utah." I'm sitting there looking at the email, confirming my appearance about two weeks later, and I'm thinking to myself, "Why would they put me on TV in Salt Lake City? I'm a middle-aged guy nobody's ever heard of. I've got a self-published book nobody's ever bought. I have no TV experience. Are they really going to do it?"

They actually did. They put me on TV in Salt Lake City, and I went there to show them how great I was going to be, and to use that as my audition tape for the *Today* show.

You know what? I sucked! It's a good thing I wasn't on the

Today show, because I would have sucked even worse. Knowing what I know now, I probably would have wet my pants. I called up the publicist and said, "Well, that was fun. Get me some more of those so I can work on getting better." She said, "Sure! How many more would you like?" I said, "Three more would be good."

I did two appearances in Sacramento, one in Phoenix and in Salt Lake City. That was four times $1,500 – that was $6,000 I spent in my first month of doing TV publicity. I showed them all to my wife and she said, "You're going to have to do a lot more TV appearances if you're going to get good enough to get on the *Today* show."

I don't know if you've ever failed visibly in front of somebody whom you were trying to impress and who you love, but it doesn't feel very good. Luckily, my wife still supported me. She said, "You can do this, but do you have to keep paying this woman to book you on these shows? Why don't you try booking yourself on these shows?"

My wife is such a genius. She really is because that was the smartest thing. It took me a couple of months to figure this out. Luckily, I'm a very determined person. Over three-and-a-half years, I've done over 61 TV appearances. That shows you my dedication to what I'm doing.

The Value of Lessons Learned

It took me a couple of months to figure out how to book myself on TV. The first year I only booked eight appearances. I did a little tour of Louisiana, Texas, Missouri, Mississippi, and I ended up with eight more appearances. By the end of the second year, I did my 32nd appearance on NBC New York. I was still the same middle-aged guy nobody had really ever heard of. I had the same self-published book – actually, it was a book that hadn't even been published yet. I booked myself on NBC New York with a book that didn't exist yet. I just had a book cover that I made. They booked me on just from having the book cover and a segment proposal – a one-page proposal.

Three years into this whole adventure, I did my 58th television appearance on the *Today* show – the show they would never book me on. Brooke Shields interviewed me. She said, "You talk about how important it is to go out of your comfort zone." I'll tell you what; this whole thing has been one more episode out of my comfort zone every single time. Believe me, going on the *Today* show, as many shows as I've been on, it was still out of my comfort zone.

I said, "That's right. I believe that life begins where your comfort zone ends." The more you challenge yourself, the more scary it is; the more difficult it is, the more you grow and the more you get out of life. I really believe all of that, and I really believe that anybody can do exactly what I have done if they just model what I've done and use the teachings.

My students have been on the *Today* show, *Good Morning America*, *Dr. Oz*, CNN. I started teaching people how to do what I do about two years ago. Since then, my students have booked more than 1,045 TV appearances, including all those big shows. It's been a huge adventure. I've won an award as the KIC Information Marketer of the Year. James Malinchak and Mike Koenigs are previous Marketers of the Year. I'm in pretty illustrious company.

Really what this is all about is creating celebrity for your personal brand, and differentiating yourself by being a celebrity using local TV news and talk show interviews, and using them to work your way up to the big opportunities like the *Today* show and *Dr. Oz* and the biggest shows in the world. Anybody can do it. If I can do it, anybody can do it. I was just a middle-aged guy with no TV experience that nobody had ever heard of. A while ago, Brooke Shields was interviewing me on the *Today* show. There you go.

Not long ago, I was at a conference, the Dan Kennedy Advanced Wealth Attraction seminar. I went out to dinner with two people who had just signed up for my programs, and two other people who were considering signing up. It was really interesting – they're all looking at me differently than they're looking at each other, I'll tell you that much.

The next morning I get a text message from one of the guys who hadn't yet signed up. He said, "Can we meet for breakfast?" I said, "Sure."

I get there and he's reading my book on his iPad. The book he's reading was my most recent book, which, by the way, this is how it came into being. The *Today* show called me up and said, "We want you to come on." I knew they wanted me to come on to talk about my *Last Year of Your Life* book, which is part of the *Greatest Book of All Time*.

The *Greatest Book of All Time* is the greatest book of all time. It's a 52-week personal transformation experience where you live as if you're going to die at the end of the year, and every single week has different challenges and explorations about what it means to be a human being, complete with audios and videos embedded in a Kindle book. You click the link in your

Kindle book, and if you've got an advanced enough iPad or Kindle Fire, it opens up a video or audio file and it starts playing off the Internet. It's amazing.

I knew that what they wanted for the Today show was something about *The Last Year of Your Life* because I'm famous for this question: "If this were going to be the last year of your life, what would you want to accomplish?" It really is a powerful question. They asked me a question on the Today show to illicit that response from me. You'll see it if you watch it. I knew that I wanted to promote my TV publicity stuff. They called me up on a Thursday. By Saturday morning, not only was I confirmed on the *Today* show for a Monday or Tuesday morning appearance, but I had also published a new book already called *Break Through Your Upper Limits on TV*, because I really believe that television publicity and everything that I've been doing is a personal growth experience.

Words of Wisdom and Vision

Like Jim Rohn used to say, "It's not the million dollars you make, it's what you become in the process of making the million dollars." It's the same thing about TV. It's not the *Today* show that is so great – it's what you become in the process of earning your way on to the *Today* show. You don't get on there unless you've earned it.

I've transformed my whole being in the process of being a guest worthy enough of receiving the call inviting me to be a speaker on the Today show. I published this Kindle book, and I published it as a print on demand paperback through CreateSpace called *Break Through Your Upper Limits on TV*.

I get down to this meeting in the restaurant in this hotel, and there is this prospect reading my book, *Break Through Your Upper Limits on TV* on his Kindle. He said, "Wow – this book is really awesome!" I said, "Thank you." We had a 30-minute meeting. At the end of this 30-minute meeting, he signs up for my $18,000 coaching program. That's what a book can do for you.

This book is a really sophisticated way of focusing your thoughts and demonstrating your command of your topic. Do you need a book in this world in order to succeed? No. Do the most successful people in the expert space have books? Yes, they all do. If you see yourself as having a future in the expert industry, if you're an author, a speaker, a coach, an entrepreneur and you want to sell coaching programs or consultations, or if you're a doctor or a lawyer, a great way to differentiate yourself from 95% of your competition, who are looking for some kind of get rich quick scheme or an easy way to get ahead, is to write a book.

Most of those people, 95% of them, are not going to have the vision for their career to say, "I should be a published author." It's easier than ever to do it. Here's the beauty of it – once you've got the book, now you can really start leveraging your positioning. You don't need a book to get on TV, but it's a lot easier to get on TV if you have a book.

A lot of times you can get on TV to talk about stuff simply because you've been on a lot of TV and you're good at being on TV – that in itself is a skill. I'm telling you, this is the smartest way you can position yourself as an entrepreneur is to go on TV and get the celebrity positioning of being an expert guest on TV on whatever topic. It really doesn't matter what the topic is; only celebrities go on TV.

Only special people go on TV. I figured out a way how to reverse engineer so that anybody can get on TV and work their way up and learn how to be a great TV guest, and build their celebrity along the way getting free marketing videos produced for them by ABC, NBC, CBS, FOX, and CW news and talk show producers along the way. It's just the best deal ever invented for marketing and positioning for any expert that there is. Anybody can do it. It's paint by numbers, basically.

As soon as you go on TV, you become an instant celebrity.

5. Find Your Authentic Success
Shari Yantes

Shari Yantes is an author and personal success coach who has been coaching, mentoring, speaking, and training for over 20 years. She spent many years in Corporate America with both Fortune 100 companies as well as family-owned businesses leading human resource departments.

Finding the most inspiration and happiness in helping others succeed and follow their dreams, Shari left the corporate world to devote herself to helping people live their dreams and find authentic happiness and success. www.shariyantes.com

My Vision

My vision is to help people find the confidence and courage to take control of their lives, so they can live an authentic life. I've always been that person who people go to. Ever since I was a little girl with other kids and then raising my kids, their friends come over and they talk to me before they talk to their parents.

I had a life that was very colorful, full of lessons, and I always wanted to help people. I always wanted to fix things; make things better. I would participate in things like Special Olympics, Girl Scouts and events to help people. Then, after school I moved into HR. I spent years helping people obtain jobs, get promotions, learn new skills, and encouraging them to go after what they wanted. I really had this passion my whole life of helping others to refocus and believe in themselves, to find their confidence and their courage to overcome obstacles and even just to give people a smile.

Growing up with lots of turmoil, I saw a lot of hurt. I wanted to fix it, but realized I couldn't fix it for everybody. I'm only in control of myself. Helping other people to see that they're in control of themselves, their destiny, and helping them find those steps to take was really rewarding for me, whether it affected me directly or not, to watch people overcome what they were going through.

Being in HR, I got to do that. Unfortunately, I had to do the bad side of HR of laying people off and what was sometimes perceived as ruining people's lives, but the reality of that was oftentimes it made it better, because they weren't where they really needed to be at that point anyway.

My Voyage

Even when we make little changes, we go through that fear and self-doubt. There are these "Can I do it? Can I make it happen?" questions coming from inside of us. Then mustering up the courage, the confidence, and believing in myself to do that. Along with that then, come your naysayers.

I had a wonderful career. I was financially doing very well, and I was very comfortable. I had status and all that other stuff, but I was miserable. I wasn't living authentically. I didn't like playing the corporate games. Really, that challenge of listening to the naysayers – "What do you think you're doing? Why would you leave that? You have a great job. Suck it up! This is what life's about. People go to work, make a living. You can have fun outside of work." I just didn't believe that.

I lost my real father when he was 51 years old, and then in 2011 my stepfather passed away at the age of 65. A few months later, I lost a sister who was 40. I always knew when I retired, I was going to be a coach and I was going to do what I called the fun side of HR. (That's what we do, we wait until we retire to live the life we want to live, right?)

In my current job, I get to do what I did in Corporate America; I just do it for individual people. After losing all those people who were important to me at such a young age, I decided that's life too short. I, in essence, retired early and started my dream job.

There are a lot of things that come with that; there are these challenges, and not just the feelings and fear-based things, but there are a lot of skills – realizing what you need and what you don't have, finding the gap and figuring out how to fill it. There were skills that I honed, and I got education on and things like that. There are others that I said, "That's not something I'm going to do," and so I hire those out. It's really finding that balance, and again I think the biggest thing is really just believing in yourself and being strong enough to stand up to the people who don't believe in you.

The Value of Lessons Learned

Some of the biggest lessons I learned that I would pass on to people are, first of all, find a routine, whatever that routine is that works for you. When you're used to going to the same place and doing the same thing over and over, when you make that shift and you're now an entrepreneur, a solopreneur, whatever the situation is, you have this freedom and flexibility, and you don't have someone holding you accountable. Hold yourself accountable. Find a routine.

Make sure that your routine includes some self-care. We get so focused on running our business. "I have to do this, I have to do that, I have to make this work …" but you can't run yourself ragged, because then you're not going to be healthy to do the rest of it.

It's also very important to surround yourself with like-minded, positive people who will support you and encourage you, who can teach you and mentor you, or who you can teach and mentor.

It is hard to make these transitions. The people who are closest to you – your family and friends – they want you to succeed, but they want you to remain as you are. They think they're trying to help when they say things like, "Gee, maybe it's better if you just go back and get a job in Corporate America. You wouldn't have so much to worry about."

What you really want and need is to be around the people who say, "You've got this – go for it! What can I do to help? What can I do to support you?"

I really want people to be their true selves; to not worry about what society, culture, media, school, parents, etc. think they should be. I want people to decide for themselves who and what they want, and to be able to live that without fear.

I think there are so many people – and I would venture to say the majority of people – who really live behind a mask; they live as to how they're expected to live. Again, that's different for everybody, because it may be that you're brought up in a certain religion where you're taught that these are the behaviors you must follow. Maybe you are told, "You will be a doctor or you will be a lawyer or you will be this or that." Mommy and Daddy are paying the bill, so that's what you do, but you're unhappy. Life is too short to be unhappy.

If I could wave my magic wand, everybody would get to live his or her life and be happy. Once I decided to make this change, was it hard? Absolutely. But am I happier and more fulfilled and more present for my family and friends now than I've ever been? Yes, I am.

Everybody would tell you I'm happier. I look better. I smile. I get to be home. I take my son to school or to a summer program. I pick him up from school every day. He goes to things with me, whether I'm doing an event or something like that. He participles. He's learning that you can do and be these things.

My daughter, who is now in her early twenties, helps me. She has been learning some business aspects of it.

Again, I'm there. I take care of my mom since my dad died. If I need to, I can run up to my mom's house. I am so much more relaxed. I wasn't sleeping well. I wasn't eating well. I'm just so much healthier all around.

Words of Wisdom and Vision

To find your purpose, the first action would be to do the background work. Do your homework and make a plan, even if you just plan a little. I also caution people, "Don't get stuck in planning and analyzing, but at least have your plan."

When I first left, people said, "What if this doesn't work? What's your plan B?" I said, "I don't need a plan B. I'm not having a plan B."

But I had a plan A. I got my coaching certification the year before I left corporate, so I planned ahead a little. That's the first thing people need to do is take a look, know what you want to do, create that road map.

Remember that you don't have to go it alone. I think we all think, "This is my company. I have to do everything." One, you can't do everything. You need help. You need guidance. You need support. The reality is, no one ever does it alone. You might create the concept, you might create the product, you might be the face of the company, but there's always somebody, something, somewhere along the line that has helped you open a door or take care of something. Surround yourself with those people, like we talked about earlier, and create that network. Get out there and get to know people.

Lastly, be honest with yourself. I think this is probably the most important thing for people is really looking inside themselves and being honest. Are you living true to yourself and who you are, and is this really what you want or is someone telling you that you need to do it?

Really ask yourself those hard questions and then live authentically, live true to yourself. If you're not being authentic, you're going to burn out. You're going to get frustrated, and everything is going to be much harder.

I do a few things daily to stay positive and keep moving forward. I meditate in the mornings and at night. Usually I fall asleep at night meditating. I thought meditation meant you had to take 20 minutes and sit still in silence with your eyes closed and your legs crossed. That's just one way to meditate. Find what works for you! You can do it in as little as a couple minutes a day. Just allow yourself that time to focus.

Have your goals, your vision posted so you see them every day. I also recommend journaling. I journal. I write. Even if it's a sentence or two, that gets it out of your head, whether that's a bad feeling or frustration, or just to say, "Wow, I'm okay."

Then, always list three things you're grateful or thankful for before you go to bed. Fill your mind with gratitude before you fall asleep.

6. Ask "Why Not" Instead Of "Why"
Gary Barnes

Gary Barnes is "America's Traction Coach." He is a high performance business and sales coach, popular international speaker, and Amazon best-selling author of six books. Gary's clients span over seven countries, and he's been featured on ABC, CBS, NBC, FOX, and PBS to name just a few.

He's the founder of Gary Barnes International, and he has created three successful businesses from the ground up. Married for over 40 years with adult sons, he has completed a world-class 40-foot firewalk, flown in a World War II P51 flyer, flown on a trapeze, completed a 75-foot bungee jump, and climbed a 14,000 foot mountain. He is a drummer and a police academy graduate.

Gary also understands dealing with adversity. He fought a life-threatening illness, and he won. He believes that your worst day is the day you meet the man or woman you could have been, and it's your choice. garybarnesinternational.com.

My Vision

Early on, I was looking at affecting millions and millions of lives, and now I have brought it back to really affecting one life at a time, and to be able to do it in a way that is meaningful to that person who I am connecting with.

The largest audience I've ever addressed was over 12,000, but I've addressed that 1 to 3 to 5-person group as well. Before I connect with whatever I'm doing and even on this interview, my focus is: If we can just touch at least one person, then having invested this time together would have been worth it, because it's that one on one that multiplies, and exponentially it creates a wave.

Sometimes we create a wave that we don't even know where it goes or where it touches later on; but because we've decided to do this and we have touched another life, that life can touch others. My vision really is to create a movement to create a synergy while I have the blessing and the opportunity to do what I do.

People have asked me when I'm going to retire. I tell people this is not what I do – *this is who I am*. My vision is to touch as many people as possible, but doing it as effectively and efficiently as I possibly can.

My Voyage

It really is an interesting journey, as I think most people's journeys are. I grew up in a family where I was told consistently, "You can't. It's not for you." I had told my mother particularly that I was going go into the ministry, and she said, "No. You have to have a call from God." I was always coming up against an obstacle of "no" before I got to do anything. I tell people that may be why I went eventually into sales, because I had to sell all the way through.

I did go into theology; my early background was theology and psychology. That really formulated a position for me that I had to conform into a box, and out of that box it just did not feel normal. I was always at odds within the structure of that box.

When I left the formal ministry, I went into business. I had gone into real estate when I was in college, because I had to support myself through college. Out of that, I formed one of the very largest high production financial planning firms in the country. Over the last 10 or 15 years, I sold that and I went into speaking and coaching full time.

The Value of Lessons Learned

For me, it was looking at the obstacles as seeds of opportunity. I believe it was Norman Vincent Peale who said that it really is the opportunities that are disguised as obstacles that give us that reaction to where we are to go to whatever that destiny is that we have chosen for ourselves. For me, it's releasing that inner desire, because I believe that desire is put there. That seed of greatness has been what Denis Waitley used to talk about. It's about allowing it to germinate and to see where it takes us.

It is a progression of obstacles that we go through. The earliest ones were: I came from a family that really didn't do things outside the box. In fact, my father, up until two weeks before he passed away, told me that I was a "dumb, fat Barnes." People hear that when I tell that story from stage and they think, "What an evil person!" But he really wasn't. It was a reflection of his own insecurity – he didn't want me to go out there, strive, be disappointed, get hurt, and be rejected.

Two weeks before he died, he reached over and took my hand and he apologized. He said, "Gary, I'm sorry." He started to see a glimpse of what I had persevered to do, even though I had some of those basic foundational beliefs given to me at an early age.

Going through business and going through economies where people said, "It's a bad economy – you can't do what you're going to do," my first year in business I grossed just under $200,000 and my wife told me it was gross. I said, "Absolutely. We have to take our expenses out of that." There were obstacles all the way along in business.

In 1988, right about the time that my businesses really started taking off, I was diagnosed with multiple sclerosis and was told that I would be dead or in a wheelchair within 10 years. That diagnosis was something that my wife had a very difficult time with, because she is a psychotherapist and her graduate work was with a community of individuals who had been diagnosed with it. She was envisioning what my end result was going to be.

I looked at the doctor and said, "Okay, what are we going to do?" He had originally given me three choices. It would have been cancer, a brain tumor, or MS. When he finally told me it was MS, I said, "Thank you." In my mind, he had given me a life sentence. Yes, there were going to be challenges. At that time, I had no feeling from the neck down. I had lost the ability to write. I had lost the ability to walk. I could walk, but if I didn't see where my feet were I'd stumble and fall. I asked him, "What can we do?"

He said, "You don't understand. You're going to be dead or in a wheelchair in 10 years. Go home and plan your life as it's virtually over."

The thing that I want to share with everyone is that whatever your obstacle is, if you don't accept it as fact, your brain looks for an opportunity to overcome. I have never said I had something. I've always said, "I was diagnosed with …"

That means that it was someone else's opinion. That doesn't mean that I didn't deal with challenges. When I speak, I make friends with all the hotel staff because I literally cannot do some of the buttons on my shirt. They adopt me, and I build new friendships. When I go back to the hotels, they embrace me; that's very cool.

The obstacles that we have in front of us, if we don't accept them as fact, then we have the opportunity to find a solution that is opposite or contrary to what the general population might think.

I have what's called "Garyisms." One of my Garyisms is "All facts are stories until they become beliefs." I have lived my life that way. That doesn't mean that everything has always turned up rosy and peachy, but I have been able to progress. I think it's normal now. Everyone has the abilities within them. It's just a matter of identifying where they truly want to go, and then allow the stimulus of whatever that empowerment is and desire to get them there. It's about giving permission to ourselves.

Words of Wisdom and Vision

Another of my "Garyisms" is "Are you a participant or are you a spectator? It's your choice."

What I came to understand about the question is that it was okay either way. I could choose to be a spectator; I could choose to be a participant – but I had to choose. If I chose to be a spectator, it was totally okay.

For me, I had realized that I had done some things in business and I had a level of success, but I had never stepped into what I call my light. When I talk about publicity and celebrity, sometimes we have this concept that if I step into the light, I'm going to steal somebody else's light. I don't believe that. I believe that if we don't step into our own light, the only thing that's going to go away is our light.

The ability to go from a spectator to a participant is one simple step. I love football and the guys in the stands and the guys on the sidelines, they're all spectators. It only takes that one step onto the field before they become a participant. For me, I step into being a participant. It's a decision every single day.

It's interesting, because some of my early work before I was a pastor, I took hospital chaplaincy. Out of the hospital chaplaincy work, we had to deal with our own mortality to the point where we had to go to our own funeral, write our own epitaph, and really deal with the idea that this life is finite. When I had the diagnosis and experience with the multiple sclerosis, it brought all of that back to me in my early thirties, this life was very, very short, and it's very precious.

A concept that I teach around and I feel very energized by is the concept of time. I no longer spend time – *I invest time*. Knowing that no matter what it is that we have, we're not guaranteed tomorrow. We're not guaranteed next year. We have plans, but if we're not investing our time right now the way that we want for a return on that investment, then we're wasting our lives, in my opinion. We're losing that "what if" possibility.

The early experiences taught me that there is not a panic urgency, but there's a deliberateness that when you sit down and do one thing, you're making a decision not to do any other possibility that was in the realm of choices. It's okay, but if we are not conscious of how we do things, then we might spend the weekend in front of the television. We may not take the opportunity to take that vacation with our family or go to the ball game with our kids, or whatever it is that's important to you.

That's where I think some of the regrets in life happen later on. We look back and think, "If I had only invested my time a little differently, what would have the results been?" I think that's the main thing that the obstacle gave me, a viewpoint at a very early age. There were only so many minutes, days, and years that we're going to have as an opportunity to be on this planet.

What legacy do we want to leave for that future generation that may not even have the opportunity to meet us? What can we start and put in place that movement, that momentum, that heritage that we can give to a future generation?

For me, it's allowing our kids – and we did this deliberately – grew up the idea of "why not" instead of "why." They've had some struggles and challenges, but they have really flourished in the things that they have chosen to do in their life, and now we're seeing it manifested in our grandchildren.

The legacy is that we have this beautiful thing called life. What is it that we are going to be able to leave as a legacy as a point of reference? People say the number one fear in the world is the fear of public speaking. I think there's another one, though, that we don't talk about – and that's the fear of being forgotten. What happens is that when we start a concept, we start a belief system within our family, when we write a book and leave a legacy and leave the stories behind us; then we are not going to be forgotten.

They may not remember our names, and that's not really that important. It's the things that we hold dear to ourselves and what has served us well, and sometimes more importantly what has not served us well. If people chose to, they do not have to make the same mistakes or create the challenges in their lives. It's being able to leave that footprint that somebody else can step into that can progress to another level even far beyond wherever I am able to go in my lifetime.

7. Power Your Dreams
Dorothy Kuhn

As Founder and CEO of Power My Dreams, **Dorothy Kuhn** works with entrepreneurial leadership teams that are *ready to be great.* If you'd love to have all the great customers you want, a wonderful culture and outstanding operations, join Dorothy at www.powermydreams.com.

My Vision

I believe trust and authenticity are the foundations of greatest, in life and business. My vision is to help busy business owners get what they've always wanted — a stronger, healthier business, happier owners and employees, great customers and clients, and most of all, less stress and more fun. The way I do this is by asking great questions, listening closely, considering proven options, and bringing you the simplest, most effective solutions that give you the business, and the life, you've dreamed of.

Trust and authentic relationships are huge in my life. This means I continually go above and beyond to find the best proven solutions, so you don't have to hunt through myriad options to find what you really need. I've done that for you.

Any business is as strong as its weakest part. My vision is for strong, wonderful businesses all across our land. Businesses that are good for their owners, employees, customers and communities.

So you have the business and the life you've always wanted. You *can* have your life back.

My Voyage

I started off life as a mystical kid, but when life threw me curveballs, I stuffed feelings, becoming an uber-geek. Physics. Math. Think *Big Bang Theory*, with mascara. I learned a lot, accomplished much. And then I noticed my life wasn't working for me. I started what Marcia Wieder describes as the journey back to self, to essence. It's been a difficult and magnificent journey. I'm so glad I did it. And glad to still be on the journey.

Being more fully human is wonderful. From my foundations in process improvement, metrics, Lean and Six Sigma, to NLP (Neuro-Linguistic Programming), Dream Coaching, EOS and WHY Coaching, the arrows in my quiver are the best available. Discarded are those that didn't make the cut.

Beyond this, I'm gifted to see the patterns of life and business. The ability to see unhelpful, unhealthy patterns, then transitioning these patterns to simple, helpful and healthy, has provided huge value, time after time. Clients' smiles on the other side change are beautiful to see.

My continuing question ... "How can we make this better?"

The challenge to get here was huge. I married in my twenties and, as marriages often are, ours was emotionally prickly, shall we say. It provided a lot of challenges, as does life. One of the things that I just absolutely had to reflect on was this: we had two beautiful children, he was the husband of my youth, and I wanted it to work out.

I stumbled into NLP. It was actually an introductory continuing education course at Southern Methodist University, here in Dallas, called *Elegant Communication.* "I could use more of that," I thought. Little did I know!

NLP is about clean communication with self, with others. Starting with self – after all, who's the person that we talk with the most? Yeah, ourselves.

I ended up taking two series of weekend workshops, Practitioner and Masters. Plus the extra offerings. (Here's that "Above and Beyond" above and beyond again!)

It gave me the ability to really make a significant belief-upgrade, in a weekend and one that I could repeat on other beliefs anytime. Nice.

A weekend a month for 16 months gave me the opportunity to go from being a bit jumpy and not breathing well, to much more myself. You know when you don't breathe well. It's hard to really make good decisions when you're not connected very well to your body, a huge resource in making well-formed decisions and making them quickly. This was the beginning of my journey back to essence.

My goal was to be the best Dorothy I could be. I knew when I was the best, most whole Dorothy, that I had the best opportunity to recover the marriage, to be a wonderful wife and mom, and be happy. I really wanted this.

I got there, through an elegant ("collaborative") route out of the marriage, recovering my relationships with every member of my family. In a different configuration.

And from this, had the courage to launch my own business, helping many clients and having the time of my life. Bringing my clients the simplest, most effective approaches, tools, belief upgrades and systems.

One way is *WHY*. A couple years ago, when I heard Simon Sinek's TED Talk, *How Great Leaders Inspire Action*, I thought, "I have got to find a way to incorporate this into my coaching. It's so clearly powerful to start with "why" you do what really drives you!"

Well, I didn't know what my "why" was, so I was slogging away on it. This past April, who showed up on Marcia's Wealthy

Visionary stage? Ridgely Goldsborough. What an amazing man. I thought, "I'm open to possibility and God provides."

Starting with "why" is Simon Sinek's great idea, and the wonderful thing that Ridgely, Dr. Gary Sanchez and that whole WHY leadership team has done is to turn this great idea into practical tools. As you know, I leave lesser methods in the dust when a superior one is ready. Business people want practical, simple tools that get *results*.

Starting with WHY gives you the ability to see clearly your deepest "filter" – the filter that informs every decision you make! Can we agree it would be helpful know this filter? Knowing this allows you to express yourself authentically, attracting your ideal clients. Who doesn't want more of these? Ideal clients are fantastic!

When your whole team knows their WHYs, they know who they can count on for more than skills. They know who they can count on for Trust, for thinking outside the box, for finding a better way, and more.

When I first saw that TED Talk, I had no idea how many ways it strengthens a business – both inside and to the world. It's amazing, simple, inspiring.

How would you discover your WHY? Most people are stuck, like I was. Wondering … what is my *why*?

Discovering your WHY has gone from impossible, to possible-in-hours, to reliable-in-minutes.

How we discover this better, faster, reliably is based in brain biology. Oh, my inner geek! Well, just a touch. Here's the short-

short. Your WHY is deeply held, in a part of your brain that doesn't do language – and makes ALL your decisions. And then there's the part of your brain that does language, analysis – a good education helps this part of the brain. But it makes NO decisions. So what's the bridge between these two?

Stories. Stories that connect us to the emotion of a specific event. And for your WHY, it's a specific interaction where you felt successful.

Our WHY Coaches are a rare breed. We're skilled at asking the right questions and listening for the subtleties. The results are delightful, transformative. More, they empower you and your business, in leadership, culture and the full customer experience.

Follow-up questions discover your HOWs, knitting them to your WHY and your WHAT, in a full message that speaks to the brain's decision-maker. Often what we call our "heart" or our "gut".

In the early days, we saw there were a variety of WHYs. After thousands were discovered, we had to ask, are there themes? Kinds? Turns out, Yes. From all those WHY success stories, we've found nine kinds of WHYs. Of course we're open to other kinds showing up. After all, when the WHY Team's Vision is "A world where everyone knows their WHY", and the world has over 7B people, it's possible.

In a crowded and noisy world, we want to clearly communicate from our beliefs so that *people who resonate* with our beliefs can see us, hear us. So they can immediately raise their hand and say, "I like you. I want to be with you. I want to be a part of your tribe." They become your raving fans. Think Apple. Harley Davidson.

Back to empowering (like raving fans isn't enough). Following-up with a recent client, they are now organizing the whole company around their WHY. Internally and externally. They're using it to get the right people in the right seats, to better understand and appreciate one another. To express who they are and what they believe to the world – to base all their marketing on it. Just like Apple. Harley Davidson. Because they want their ideal clients, their piece of our 7B people, to instantly get them!

By contrast, you can see how wasteful it is to spend money marketing with normal, standard expression. Pick any industry. They'll advertise like this one, for dentists: "We love teeth. We straighten, whiten, and fill teeth. We do veneers and crowns. We have a professional staff and three convenient locations. Come see us."

How does this distinguish them from anyone else? What else would they say, "we have unprofessional staff and inconvenient locations?" I don't think so!

What if instead, they took one minute to say, "At Sanchez Dental Associates, we believe life is better with great teeth." We also know there are so many people living below their potential. They are living a life of quiet desperation, because of their teeth. They're embarrassed or they're in pain. They don't like to smile. They don't like to be social. They really aren't living. This usually happens because of fear, and it doesn't have to be that way. So our vision is to give these people their lives back. The way we do this is by providing a safe, pain-free experience that alleviates their stress and allows them to get the smile they've always wanted. So they can be who they're meant to be. And that's what we do. I'm Dr. Gary Sanchez. If this sounds like your story, then give us a call at 555-1212."

The results? Since this radio ad started running, every year at Dr. Sanchez' office has been their *best year ever*. Year after year, for over five years. Who are the people who show up? They feel that Dr. Sanchez was speaking *to them*. They are his raving fans.

On to when you *don't* have the right people in the right seats. Not a happy situation. You know it, because *they're* not happy. Not particularly productive. You've seen it. You may have been *in* this situation.

Top managers don't want to loose valuable expertise and experience. It's expensive to rebuild. But what to do? Where to move them? Wouldn't it be great to have a guide? Knowing their WHY is a huge help, as some WHYs are a great fit for a given role, where others often are not.

Can we agree that great culture and great customers make for a great business? I think so!

What about outstanding operations? Remember, I'm the *what's the pattern* gal, and we know your business runs only as well as the slowest or weakest part.

So, of course, outstanding operations made simple.

EOS stands for Entrepreneurial Operating System, and one of the things I absolutely love about EOS is that it leverages so much of what I had done in my career in Fortune 500 industries, with a *twist*. It's simple, and well suited to smaller businesses of 10-to-300 people. Just right.

Most people who have a business are great at what they do, but less skilled on the business-side. In other words, often people work *in* the business a lot. And rarely work *on* the business. Are you working *in* your business pretty much all the time?

To work on the business takes "stepping out" of the business for a time. Weekly, this is 60-90 minutes. What to do in this time? Running a top-flight meeting can be simple, but few know how. Other, occasional meetings are needed for longer term planning and problem solving. There's a happy rhythm of solving problems enjoyed by healthy businesses.

Wouldn't it be great to solve bothersome issues so they go away? Would "gone forever" be good? You bet!

When you solve the issues of your business at the root, your team looks at them, prioritizes them, and solves them at the root cause. Not just the symptom. Can you imagine how much time you get back on your calendar?! Reducing your firefighting week-by-week, quarter-by-quarter, is a Great way to run a business.

Back to my love of systems and patterns of healthy versus unhealthy. It's just indescribably delicious to help any business, any organization to transition from where they are into a healthier pattern. It's seeing the joy and happiness on their faces. Wow.

The Value of Lessons Learned

The most valuable thing is to really be able to step back and look at life as though it were somebody else's for the moment. Just to pretend that you're looking at your own life, and ask, "What's not working well? How can I be different? What can I do differently next time, to make it better? What would get the kind of results that I want?" This ability to have an arm's length reflection on one's own life is huge and powerful.

Not only this, but having a good coach / mentor / guide. It's essential. When you're the runner, you cannot also be the coach. A good outside perspective is essential to your success.

For me, building this habit started with NLP. Our trainer/coach, Susan Stageman, was fantastic. And our wonderful MasterMind continued for five years – because it made a difference. Since, through Marcia Wieder's work, I've added meditation, active dialogue, and other practices – Always with a MasterMind.

These practices have a delightfully spiritual aspect. Most mornings I get up and meditate for 15 minutes. It gives me the opportunity to calm my shot-out-of-bed spirit. One of the things I love about this spiritual practice is, regardless of one's theology, it calms the mind, gets you in touch with the divine, however you hold that or not, and lets you rest into the day in a way that sets you up for calm, measured success, instead of the frantic that most of us do in our over-stimulated society.

I was meditating just earlier this morning. When I finished, I picked up my journal and just jotted down all the things that came up. For me, that's a conversation with God. I ask a question, I say hello, and I just listen for the response.

Whatever it is, it is. I jot it down. Sometimes it's more philosophical. Today it was very practical. It's a list of things that needed to be done, and one of them was to get prepared for this interview. I had prepared previously, with a bit to finish, so I did it.

Healthy spiritual practices have powered my success. The magic for me in knowing my WHY, in meditating, and more, is to get in touch with the part of me that can stop me. For its own good reasons, this part can sometimes stop me from progress. It's a common human situation you may recognize! Sometimes my head and my heart are heading different directions. Not good for progress. Intentional spiritual practice helps get these "lined up".

Intention aligned with action is powerful. You can go faster, be more on point, and get your results more calmly and more quickly.

Words of Wisdom and Vision

In addition to knowing my WHY and the skill for outstanding operations, having a good spiritual practice is essential. I've mentioned most of the ones I use regularly. I've added them one-by-one over the past 10 years, finding ways to make them fit in a busy schedule. Why do it? I wake up every day feeling like I'm 30.

Here's my full list: Knowing my WHY and using it throughout my life and business. Yoga. Meditation. Active dialogue. Being in nature, walking the dog. Eating organic, mostly veggies, avoiding grains. Going to the gym. Looking at me you wouldn't guess I lift weights. But I do. The endorphins are awesome! And lots of water.

Find the ones that work for you. Get a good coach. So you can build the business – and the life – of your dreams. Everywhere I speak, I find people with dreams, aspirations, and longings. Every business starts with a big idea, a dream. Your combination of spiritual practice and practical solutions will help YOU power YOUR dreams.

Cheers!

8. Get the Key Concepts to Success
Chaffee-Thanh Nguyen

Chaffee-Thanh Nguyen is an international speaker, author, and business and success coach. He holds a Bachelor of Science in Industrial Engineering from the University of Illinois at Urbana-Champaign.

After college, he worked with Corporate America for over 11 years as an engineer and certified project manager and senior IT business analyst. Using his corporate experience, he went on to start businesses in real estate investing, networking marketing, Internet marketing, and financial services.

His passion in helping others achieve their highest potential in both business and in life is what he's all about. As a refugee himself, Chaffee is committed to helping others and giving back. He's very active within his community, serving within the Jaycees as a 10th Degree Jaycee, US Jaycee Senator, and JCI Certified National Trainer. For more information, visit his website at www.keyconceptcoaching.com

My Vision

My passion is to help people find their highest potential. I found out at a young age that we're capable of doing so much more than we're taught, whether it's in school or at home; and if people just lived their passion and worked consistently to achieve their dreams, we could accomplish so much more as a society.

My Voyage

In 1975, I arrived in the United States from a third world country. As a refugee from Vietnam, I grew up very poor. My family was a welfare family. We were fortunate to be a welfare family though. I say that because coming from a third world country, I don't know if I would be surviving today. So being on welfare in the United States was a step up.

We came over to this country with nothing. My parents took my siblings and me over to a different country. They left behind all their friends, their family, and everything they knew. We didn't speak the language, did not know anyone, and had nothing except for the clothes on our backs to start a new life.

I was very young at the time so I didn't understand what was going on, although I realized while growing up that there was more to life. I realized that just because I saw my parents working so hard, and compared to my friends, my family did not have a lot. I grew up knowing that there was more in life for us, so I worked really hard.

My father's mantra back in the day (and this is common to a lot of people I believe) was work hard, go to school, get good grades, and get a job. All my life growing up, that's what I did. I went to school; I got good grades, and worked really hard. I got that job. I got that degree as an engineer.

After getting my engineering degree and getting that job, I worked hard again for another 11 years in the corporate world. What I discovered during that time period was my passion was not to be working as an engineer in the corporate world. It just wasn't what I enjoyed doing. Even worse, it was a struggle; a struggle to wake up and actually go to work; a struggle to get things done; a struggle to focus and perform at my highest potential. I think a lot of people can relate to that. Waking up, going to work every single day and putting your hours in just to pay the bills isn't really a way to make a living. It isn't really a way to live your life, shall I say, unless that's what you're passionate about, unless that's what you enjoy; which for me, it wasn't.

For me, it was important to start discovering new things and start doing new things. That's when I made the transition to starting my own business, and really searching what I loved to do and what I enjoyed doing. I eventually found out that I loved helping people and coaching people to succeed in business and life!

After you reach a certain level of success in your own life, then it's important to help others reach that level of success as well. That's what I believe it's really about, which is achieving success for yourself first and then helping others achieve their successes. The more success you achieve, the more success you can help others achieve.

What I found out about coaching is that it's always different with everybody you talk to. One of the most powerful things about coaching is it's not just about the student or the client or the business or whatever it is that you're coaching – it's that you can learn so much from those individuals you're helping. You learn so much from both being coached and actually coaching.

Take, for example, the martial arts. I took 9 years of martial arts when I was growing up. Part of my martial arts training required me to teach the techniques and strategies to other students, young and old. And while I was fairly good at martial arts, until I started teaching martial arts, I really didn't fully understand it. It's the same thing with coaching. It's the same thing with business and life. Until you start working with other individuals and teaching certain concepts, you don't really understand those concepts yourself, even though you might be implementing or applying those concepts in your life.

It's that deep fundamental understanding of those concepts that really help you move forward as an individual and allows you to help other people move forward, because you have to explain it to them in a manner that they understand. I love coaching for the fact of, not only do I get to learn great things about individuals, but I get to know the students, and I get to know different people in their lives and their experiences. I get to help them move forward, and I get to help them see the light bulb go on above their head and get that breakthrough and that "ah-ha" and really start living their life versus just experiencing life happened by them.

One of the biggest things I teach is integration. It's a word I don't think people understand, because we're constantly being taught "balance" in our life. We're taught that you should balance your professional life with your personal life, and you should balance your spiritual life and your financial life, and all these different lives.

When you think of balance you think of a scale, and you think of two sides of something. You think of different things, and instead what I like to teach is integration. What I mean by "integration" is that if you look at the ultra successful individuals, the people that are really doing what they love, there's really no balance in their life because they've integrated everything. They do what they love and they love what they do. Their work, their professional life is their personal life. Their friends and their family, they surround themselves by those individuals that love what they do as well.

When you're doing what you love and integrate your personal, your professional, your financial, your emotional, and your spiritual lives, then you become one whole individual. That's the message that I really love to tell people; that you don't have to do a job just to pay the bills so that you can do what you love. If you follow your passions and find a way of monetizing those passions in such that it's not a "job" and that you're still doing what you love and you make money at it, then you can start doing even more of what you love.

You might have heard of the saying, "Follow your passion and the money will come." That's true to a degree. You do want to follow your passion, only you have to be smart about it. You want to follow your passions, and then find ways of monetizing that by sharing your passion with other individuals who are passionate about the same thing. It's not just going out there and doing what you love – it's finding and sharing that passion. The more you share your passion, the more people that buy into your vision, the more successful you will be.

That's the main message that I want to get out there. It's about integration. It's about integrating your lives together and following your passion and doing what makes you tick and what makes you move forward. By doing that, not only will you be much happier, you'll spread your passion and make a lot of other people happier as well.

The Value of Lessons Learned

Let me share one of the simplest things to do to start integrating your life. Most people don't even really think about it. The simplest thing to do is just take out a sheet of paper and just draw a big T across it, splitting the paper into two sides.

On the left side above the line write, "Things I Love To Do". Below the line, write down everything that you love to do. Whatever it is, whatever your passion is, whatever skill set that you have that you just love to do. Just write down whatever comes to mind.

Then you want to rank each of those items one through ten or one through whatever. The best thing, the thing that you love the most is number 1. The thing that you love second is number 2. The thing that you love third is number 3. And so on.

On the right side, above the line write, "Things I'm Really Good At". Then below the line, write down everything that you're good at doing. If you're good at running, if you're good at writing, if you're good at event planning, swimming, singing – whatever it is that you're good at doing, write that on the right side. Now rank the items here; the thing that you're the best at, that you do better than anybody else, that you're the top of the top, that's number one. The second thing, second, etc.

Now you have two lists. One side is something that you're great at, and the other side, something that you love to do. Now comes the fun part. You want to see if you can match the two.

Let's say for example you love writing books; only on the other side, your skill set isn't writing – your skill set is maybe telling stories. If you can match those two together, then you can develop a path to generating income.

Now, what will happen a lot of times is the thing that you love the most is not necessarily the thing that you're good at. What you'll find is that sometimes the thing that you're the best at might be fifth on the things that you enjoy doing.

It's a matter of matching your skill set to your passions. When you can find something that's fairly high – let's say you can match a 2 to a 3, that's a potential avenue for you to start following and going down a path of doing something that you enjoy doing that you can monetize.

What happens when we hear the words, "starving artist" or somebody that's struggling, is that they're doing what they love. They're doing their highest passion – only they're not really good at it from a business side or they're not really good at it from a skill set side, so they don't understand how to monetize it. By combining what you enjoy doing with what you are good at doing, that's something that you can monetize. That's something that you can make happen. By doing that, the more income you start to generate, the more you can start following those higher passions.

Words of Wisdom and Vision

I'd actually like to end with a quote by Robin Roots. Robin Roots is the individual who wrote a book called *The Success Principles of the Three Little Pigs*. It's just a simple quote that says, "It's not what you don't have – it's what you think you need that keeps you from being successful in life."

What most people need to understand is that everything they need to succeed, everything they need to achieve their highest potential is already inside. It's already within them. They already have it. They were born with the skills, the talents, and the energy that they need to succeed.

It's already there. They just need to bring that out. They just need to let it flow instead of holding themselves back because they think they need something. By letting your innate skills flow, you'll start living such a great, happier life by just following your passions and using the skills that you were born with. You don't need anything else other than what you have.

That's really the most important thing that people need to understand. They have all the greatness they need to live a life of passion already inside of them; they just need to tap into their inner strength and start living to their highest potential. Start living a life of passion and start celebrating their life!

9. Learn Before You Launch
Barbara Bamba

After being stuck behind her computer for more than 57,000 business hours researching "Over-Consuming" information products, trying to figure out how to "successfully" market numerous FAILED start-ups, **Barbara Bamba** became even more determined to launch a successful business — following a divorce and foreclosure, which left her broke, broken, and homeless and having to move back home at the age of 45, *without* all of her 3 younger children in tow – due in part to her refusal to "get a real job!"

It was in that defining moment that Barbara, decided to study the marketing of only the top 5% successful online women entrepreneurs; who had thrived during their start-up years and who had earned 6-figures plus incomes.

That is when Barbara discovered that the secret to avoid getting stuck behind your computer during your "time-sensitive" pass or fail start-up years, trying to figure out "how-to market" in this age of TMI or TOO MUCH INFORMATION is to "Learn "BEFORE" You Launch!   www.LearnBeforeULaunch.com

My Vision

My vision is to help purpose-driven entrepreneurs, who don't know where to start when it comes to marketing "their unique calling" in this age of TOO MUCH INFORMATION avoid getting stuck behind their computers, figuring "it" out, through "trial & error" – during the most critical time in their business – their first 2 start-up years.

My Voyage

After opting out of the traditional workforce in 2001 to become a work-from-home mom who sought to achieve work-life balance on my own terms, the majority of my time was spent behind my computer, trying to get 100% clarity on how to market the numerous business ventures I'd start.

Instead of me getting the word out about my new businesses, filling my sales pipeline with qualified, leads, prospects and referrals and converting prospects into clients, this was me: I was stuck behind my computer, day-after-day, from sunup to sundown surfing the internet for answers. The only time I would take breaks was when I had to "put on my mommy hat" and tend to the needs of the kids.

I was frustrated, confused and overwhelmed with information products. I would gather, collect and "Over-Consume" free and low cost information products, looking for the secrets to success.

I was busy all of the time – but not very productive. I'd stay up late at night, forfeiting valuable sleep time "tweaking and editing" stuff, trying to get "it" perfect before putting "it" out there.

My feet would swell from sitting too long. I was 100lbs overweight and I'd think about working out, but just couldn't find the time to fit a workout in.

Over a 12-year period, I wasted precious time that I can never get back and over 57,000 business development hours learning about various marketing strategies, but never stuck with any of them long enough for me to see results.

One positive thing about learning a lot of information is that you end up being academically smart ... but when you don't execute, implement or apply action to what you learn, you stay stuck, struggle and often times fail due to inaction.

You might ask, "Well, Barb, if you were so smart ... why didn't you take action?"

"And I'd say, that's a fair question, and here's my honest answer: I lacked the confidence in myself to do so. You see, I had a lot going on at the time."

I was recently divorced, due to my refusal to "get a real job" or accept a polygamous marriage arrangement.

My estranged husband stopped paying the mortgage and allowed our home to go into foreclosure to sever ties with me so that he could move on with his new life and new wife.

I had to move back home, into the backroom of my mother's 3-bedroom row house in the city, at the age of 45 without all my my children in tow.

I was surrounded by family members who didn't believe in me or my highly ambitious goal of earning 6-figures or more through entrepreneurship.

My mother, who had the worst scarcity mentality I had ever witnessed, would limit our showers to 3-4 minutes because if she heard the water running any longer, you'd have to listen to her rant for about an hour about her high bills.

One of my biggest "naysayers" was a friend who worked at the state psychiatric hospital in Rochester, NY. She personally diagnosed me as having a "grandiose personality disorder." She tried to convince me to put my "Big Dream" of becoming financially free on the back burner and in the meantime get a "Real" job!

From the outside looking in, my life did look pretty desperate to the "naysayers" as they could see that I was stuck and wasting my time!

I remember the day I had to apply for "cash assistance" at the welfare office in my mom's neighborhood.

As I sat there on the front row watching the other consumers come and go, I wondered to myself, "How many of them had a million dollar plan that could liberate them from poverty and the need for welfare?"

That was the day I knew that something was seriously wrong with me.

As I sat there, I thought to myself, "How could a highly ambitious, smart and talented woman like me be trapped inside the body and life experience of a person I didn't aspire to be?"

It was the worst feeling in the world – the knowing that my children and I deserved a better life, yet I couldn't make it happen for us.

I felt so out of place. I knew that I belonged on stage somewhere delivering messages of hope and inspiration to crowds of people, as I always dreamed of being a professional speaker.

I felt I was here for a bigger purpose. I knew I was here to serve others in a big way. I'd sometimes pray and ask God, "Why didn't He just create me to be a normal person who could graciously accept mediocrity?"

But the passion inside of me would not let up. I was determined to break through the subconscious programming that had subjected me and my kids to a life of fear, uncertainty, instability, scarcity, poverty and financial boundaries.

That was the day I decided to research only the top 5% of women entrepreneurs who were earning 6-figures or more, as those were the successful women I aspired to be like.

The Value of Lessons Learned

As I began studying successful online women entrepreneurs, I was looking for the differences between them and me. I was looking for what gave these successful women an advantage over me. What were they doing, right that I wasn't? That is when I discover what I now refer to as The 5% Secret Start-Up Marketing Advantage.

They all seemed to serve the same target market. They all spoke the same marketing language. They all used the same high profile marketing strategies. They all knew each other. They all promoted each other's products, programs and services. They all gave each other third-party endorsements through testimonials that lent credibility. They all had step-by-step systems, blueprints, formulas, boot camps and membership programs that I couldn't afford. They all knew how to sell without being "sale-sy." They all were running businesses on autopilot, like well-oiled machines. And they were running these thriving businesses "from home," with children in tow – in the worst economy I've ever seen.

And that is when the title "Learn Before You Launch" dropped into my spirit.

It was my duty and newfound mission to help other heart-centered, mission-driven entrepreneurs stop or avoid getting stuck behind their computers trying to figure out "how-to market" during their time-sensitive, pass or fail start-up years so that they too can get out there and start serving the people they were sent here to serve.

You see I wasn't alone. I was just bearing my cross, so that I could in turn help others avoid wasting their precious time, unique gifts and valuable business development hours.

Many were stuck behind their computers over-consuming information products, also known as "Bright Shiny Objects" – as they'd confess "not knowing" where to start when it comes to marketing in this age of "far too many marketing options."

I also learned that 95% of entrepreneurs were struggling financially and earning less than $100k in gross annual revenues. I learned that 80% of start-up entrepreneurs flat-out fail within their first 2 years in business, often times, due to a lack of clients and sales, while only 5% are successful.

So what I did was create a coaching program entitled LearnBeforeULaunch to help heart-centered, start-up entrepreneurs discover and develop The 5% Secret Start-Up Marketing Advantage.

I take them through the: who, what, when, where, why, how much, and how to.

Who are your assigned clients? That's an essential you need to know before you start any business. Who are your assigned clients? Meaning there are clients out there that will do business with you, but if you're not communicating in a way that they resonate with you or can find you, you're not going to make that connection. As a result of lack of clients and sales, you fail during the start-up years.

Then there's the what. What should you be saying in your sales conversations specifically when you only have seconds to capture a prospect's attention? Many entrepreneurs go to networking meetings, and they wing it when asked the million dollar question: "So, tell me, what do you do?" When the entrepreneur is neither consistent nor confident in their sales communication, prospects can pick up on that.

Then there's the when should we be out there marketing? A lot of entrepreneurs don't market because they're either serving clients one on one, or they're stuck behind their computers learning how-to.

Then there's where you should focus your marketing dollars, when there are so many options. You've got Facebook marketing, Twitter marketing, YouTube marketing, video marketing, SEO marketing, SMS marketing – who knows?

Then there's why you'll need to "exalt" your marketing to serve your "assigned clients" at a much higher level.

Then you need to know how much you're worth and how much to charge for your work so that you can confidently communicate your value in the marketplace and confidently quote your fees especially for your premium work.

Then finally, the entrepreneur needs to learn how to stand out and get the word out in the most crowded, look alike, small business marketplace in American History -- where everybody's a speaker, author, trainer, consultant or coach.

I am super passionate about helping my "assigned clients" learn all these things before launching their products, programs, practices, events and services. I don't want them wasting valuable business development hours during their start-up years, because if they do, the clock is going to run out like it has for so many others, as well as myself.

I believe that's why the small business failure rate within the first two years is so high. It's a goal of mine to see if I can decrease it just a tad bit or a lot. Let's see if we can bring those numbers down.

Words of Wisdom and Vision

Instead of competing in the marketplace on price or becoming a commodity, I think we have to exalt our marketing to show that we are the specialists in our specific niches, and go out there and attract our "assigned clients" through our own authentic voices.

The top 5% do this very well and more of us heart-centered entrepreneurs need to join them in the ranks. Our "assigned clients" are staying stuck, struggling and failing in their lives, careers, businesses, finances and relationships because we're not showing up.

If I didn't get out there with my message, can you imagine how many people would continue to stay stuck, struggle and fail during their start-up years, as a result of me not showing up?

Please, answer the call.

10. Discover Your Passion
Donald Gilbert, Ph.D.

Donald Gilbert, Ph.D. began his career as an ordained minister. He is passionate about helping others, and gifted in serving and teaching. In 2002, he had the opportunity to begin New Life Clinic in Iowa, and New Life Counseling and Consulting was born. After 33,000 hours of face-to-face counseling, he expanded his professional expertise by becoming certified through the John Maxwell team.

New Life is in the process of extending its reach through leadership training and professional growth in the spheres of both church and business. Donald offers workshops, seminars, mastermind groups, lunch and learn, keynote speaking, and coaching, aiding personal and professional growth through study and practical application of John's proven leadership methods. www.newlife-counseling.com

My Vision

Back in my twenties, I went into the ministry. As I began to experience what that was like, I began to see that speaking to a group is one thing, but also getting into a person's life and getting to know that person one-on-one and doing some personal coaching was really much more effective.

As I began to look at where I was and where I would like to go, I realized there was a lot of learning, a lot of training, and a lot of things that I needed to do to prepare for that. It's been a real process of recognizing not only my passion, but also understanding what I would say are my gifts or my experience and skills would lead me into a specific, more niche market, or being able to help people on a much more personal level. I've been able to do that.

Out of the outgrowth of that, I've come full circle to say, "Now that I've done that and I have a lot more expertise and a lot more that I think I can offer people." I really enjoy speaking that goes along with the outgrowth of the personal experience with people one-on-one, so many years and so many hours. It's just come full circle for me. Being passionate about being able to teach people, mentor people, coach people, encourage and motivate people to discover their passions as I did and to get to the place where as I say, "Discover them, develop them, so you can disseminate them."

My Voyage

I look back on my life, and the first 30 years was really more about changing the way I think about myself and began to understand who I really was. I think that was the first obstacle, to really get to know myself at a deeper level, to be encouraged by a variety of what I would term mentors in my life – people who have spoken encouragement and truth into my life. That was the first obstacle that actually began to change my thinking about myself.

I grew up thinking that I was stupid. I actually performed down to what I thought of myself. It took a while for me to really begin to change my thinking and recognize, "I really can learn, so I'm really not stupid." The first major obstacle was to really have a different view of myself. I find that's true of a lot of people when we get into the place where we really don't know where we're going – we don't have confidence in who we are.

I think the second obstacle was I had to realize that I had to go back to school and get better training. Once I began to think that I could learn, I had to go back and actually do the learning, so the obstacle there was just spending six-and-a-half years of my life in school with my wonderful wife's backing, support, and encouragement. We had four little kids at the time; I was working a full-time job, going to school full time, and six-and-a-half years was a long time. It was an investment into my life.

From that, I had a series of some major health issues. When I was 40 years old, two years after I got my Ph.D., I broke my neck. That was an obstacle of coming through that whole physical process, but that was really more of a challenge to say, "Okay, you've gone through this stage and you've gone through the second stage, and now there's another obstacle. What are you going to do with that? Are you going to stop? Are you going to continue to grow? Are you going to work through that?"

The Value of Lessons Learned

Now, I tell people my 40 to 50 was just a re-evolution — a reinventing of who I am, where I'm going and deciding — this was an obstacle, but I could get through it. Now it's come full circle because I have a successful practice; I have a successful business. Now it's about mentoring, giving back to people, encouraging people who are younger, who are still stuck and may say, "I don't know who I am or what I can do. What's my real passion of life?" I can encourage them by saying, "I've been through a lot of different things. If I can do it, so can you."

I had to learn perseverance. If you don't persevere, you never really succeed. I also learned that failure was not a problem; that failure was really about learning. What I've come up with in my life is the recognition that it's the process and the journey of learning from your failures.

Dr. John Maxwell wrote a book some time ago called *Failing Forward*. One of the concepts that I learned from that was looking at my life and saying, "Failure is not the end. Failure is just simply a stepping-stone of learning to be successful." Everybody who failed has succeeded if they learn from it. You only really fail if you stop learning. I think that was one of the obstacles that I had to go through, and that was one of the lessons I learned.

I think the other thing is that in that process when I broke my neck, there was some time where I pretty much had to rely upon those around me. It was about recognizing that in not allowing others to help you and not asking for help, you can't succeed in this journey. Really, it is about building community. It's about helping others. It's about giving back.

I remember one guy who told me, "I want to help you, but I need you to tell me what you need." In my pride, I said, "I can't do that." The words that I still remember that really helped me through that were when he said, "If you don't allow me to help you, you rob me of a blessing."

One of the things I learned in that process was there are people out there who are willing to help others; and if we say "no" or we don't ask for help when we really, truly need it, then we are robbing them of a blessing of helping. It's just a really powerful truth in my life that I just learned these principles and I learned to try to live by them; as I live by them, blessings and so many things have come my way because of that.

Words of Wisdom and Vision

I think one of the first things I would tell people is, "Don't just do nothing. Someone once said that you can't steer a parked car. You have to start moving in a direction." The first thing I would tell people is, "Do something." Figure out a direction, take a step, ask someone who maybe has been there, who is willing to give you some encouragement, some mentoring. Find a mentor. Ask someone to help you in that process. The truth is that a want is simple a wish without action. You have to take a step in some direction; otherwise, you will never steer anywhere. You will just sit still.

If you were moving in some direction, you have to at least have some goal in mind. It may not be where you end up. You may even change those goals as you go through the process.

The second thing is, "What's your vision of where you want to be? Here's point A – where's point X, Y, or Z? Where is it that you want to end up?" It doesn't mean that's where you're going to end up, but you have to have some vision, some idea. I think somewhere in the Bible it says that people perish without a vision. What's your vision? That's the second question.

I had a vision back when I was 30, and I am still working and accomplishing the vision that was set before me that I set out when someone challenged me, "Write down 150 things that you would like to accomplish before you're X" (50 years of age, for instance, when I was 30). What are 150 things that you want to do? I think there was a movie called *The Bucket List* that used that same philosophy or the same question.

So the second step is, where do you want to end up? The third step is, where are you now, and what is one thing that you can do to move you in that direction? Then simply start reading books, start asking people who have actually done what you want to do, and start interviewing people who have been successful. One of the first things that I learned was talk to people who have actually done it. Talk to successful people and ask them how they got started.

It's just recognizing that if you want to have something, you have to have a vision. The main thing is you have to go through that process of preparing yourself, which is typically learning. It's talking to other people who have been there, what have they done, getting a mentor to help you and hold you accountable, to move you in that direction. Those would be the things that I would tell people where to start.

11. Change Your Brain for Success
Dr. Simone Ravicz

Dr. Simone Ravicz is a Certified business and life coach, brain expert, speaker and an International Best-selling author. Dr. Simone Ravicz has a Ph.D. in Clinical Psychology and a MBA, which have allowed her to maximize her knowledge of human behavior and business. She worked as a psychologist for years before making the move to coaching, which she feels allows her to spread her inspirational messages to more people.

Dr. Ravicz has been studying neuroscience for the last ten years. She helps her clients, small business owners and entrepreneurs, learn how to make positive changes in the structure and functioning of their brains. Her clients experience powerful transformational shifts and are freed to move forward taking limitless strides toward business and personal success and joy. www.successbraincoach.com

My Vision

My vision actually came to me very, very early in life. My parents were anthropologists, so my brothers and I spent much of our youth traveling around the world. I was exposed to a huge variety of things. I saw beauty, kindness, and caring, and I saw poverty, violence, and death. I learned that everybody has value. I was so fascinated with watching people and how they interacted and what they said.

My Voyage

First, I wanted to be an animal behaviorist, but I shifted that to being a psychologist, studying human beings rather than animals. My vision became to use my passion and persistence to empower and inspire others to optimize their full potential, love themselves, and love others.

I think that was because I had seen really quite a lot of suffering in a lot of other countries, and things that were not, let's say, fair. I know life isn't fair, but there was a lot of inequity out there. At the same time, I saw what could happen when people really lived the lives that they wanted to live, and it was such a beautiful thing. I wanted to be part of helping with that.

The Value of Lessons Learned

I was for the most part on a single track, but I made some significant departures. I studied psychology in undergrad, but then I went into business. I went into the hospitality industry and real estate. I thought that was the thing to do. In the early '80s, everybody was about making a lot of money and working in business, so I followed suit. I even pursued getting my MBA.

I worked in business for quite a while. I did well. I was successful, but I did not feel fulfilled at all. I spent a lot of time just wondering why I was doing what I was doing, and that there had to be something better in life.

I finally decided, even though I had a lot of education, that I would go back for some more. I did go back and I got my Masters and my Ph.D. in clinical psychology. I really wanted to be prepared the best I could be to fulfill my vision of helping others.

I see now that the departures weren't a waste of time or lost time. Now, as I'm doing coaching, these business experiences are really invaluable in helping me because I do focus on helping small business owners and entrepreneurs. It's come full circle, and that does help me.

I did have another major challenge that came up. It was because I was really a major Type A and a perfectionist. I used to drive myself so hard in running my busy business. I think that from experiencing a great deal of stress, I brought on some illnesses.

I got really sick; I was hospitalized. My family was called two times to say goodbye to me, but I managed to make it through. I was released with a diagnosis of multiple illnesses. The recovery for a couple years was really slow, but I decided that I wasn't just going to lie around and mope.

I felt at such a loss. I felt I had lost myself because I was so used to doing — that's how I had defined myself — but I couldn't "do" at that time. I decided to start studying Eastern alternative and Western modes of healing and techniques, and I designed a program that I followed. It was very successful. I got better and better; and at the end of that, I was able to realize a lot about stress and how I had brought it on myself.

The impact of stress on us is how we choose to perceive it. I actually wrote a book that was called *High On Stress*. It talked about positive stress and how we can see things as a challenge and not a threat. That allowed me to really get back into the swing of things. I worked in psychology for some more years, and then I decided to go into coaching.

I don't think you can separate the two because psychology is such a part of coaching, but the role of a psychologist is different from the role of a coach. You lead more when you're a psychologist. You're more in control. With coaching, it's more of a co-creative process. You're walking on a journey together. You offer suggestions. It's up to the person to follow them.

I like helping people develop or rediscover their own motivation and seeing them become empowered to pursue their path. Also, with coaching, I felt that I could inspire and help a lot more people than I could with psychology. As a coach, I also do public speaking. I'm able to do webinars and things of that nature, so I'm able to reach out and touch more people that way. That was one of the main reasons for the switch.

It was somewhat difficult to leave the world of psychology. I loved it so much, but I think I was ready for the change. I had worked with some people who were very, very ill, and I was fortunate to be able to help them quite a bit. As I said, I wanted to have a broader range of people that I could work with, and see people really be able to optimize their lives and obtain the fulfillment and the joy, and follow their passions. That really motivated me further to make the switch.

I also have learned so much from when I became ill. I learned so much more about enjoying the process and being in the here and now and being more mindful, less judgmental. I wanted to pass that lesson on to people, because I see and work with people all the time. People, who have so much negative self-talk going on and self-criticism that just paralyzes them, and it's so unnecessary. I wanted to be able to send that message out from what I had learned from my illnesses.

I've been studying neuroscience for quite some time and I'm combining that with coaching. I'm helping people make changes in their brains which then affect their thinking, feelings, behavior, and really help them to move forward and get rid of the fears, the anxiety, and the depression. Through focusing on and repetition of positives, people can actually makes changes in the structure and functioning of their brains so that they don't need to experience those emotions anymore and their performance, productivity, success, and happiness increase.

Words of Wisdom and Vision

Examples of brain changes or neuroplasticity are evident in people who practice mindfulness meditation. After a couple of months, people studied showed greater left frontal activation. This is important because the left hemisphere is the positive side of the brain. These people reported improved moods and greater engagement with their work. Meditators also developed thicker prefrontal cortexes related to memory, decision-making and problem solving.

People who meditate have the experience of having much more emotional equanimity, peacefulness and positivity. I've experienced that myself, and so have a lot of the people with whom I've worked who've started doing meditation.

Another simple example is using visualization. If say you're going to go do some public speaking and you're very anxious about it, if you visualize yourself doing it over and over, professionally, smoothly and ending well, you greatly increase the odds that the results will be consistent with that. The brain can't tell the difference between visualization and reality. Brain changes and your experience make it much more likely you'll perform optimally when you do speak.

As I mentioned, I also felt that when I was sick I had really lost parts of myself, but they were parts, such as the need to be perfect and the need for approval, that I really didn't need and which were unhealthy. I learned to really live much more in the here and now, be more focused, and to be less judgmental of myself. I'd love to pass that lesson on to other people, because people really need to develop self-compassion. Wonderfully, greater self-compassion leads to greater compassion for others.

Self-compassion is an easier, kinder way of being. If you're interested in success, self-compassion is even more predictive of success than is self-esteem!

12. Build Your Wealth
Paul Lawrence Vann

Paul Lawrence Vann, Certified Expense Reduction Consultant (CERC); M.S. Contract & Acquisition Management; M.A. Business Management; and B.A. Business Administration. He is President and Founder of Wealth Building Academy, LLC. Paul has over 34 years of financial expertise to include financial management, cost analysis, budget analysis and expense reduction experience.

Today Paul works with small to midsize businesses to assist them in understanding how to identify savings they're not aware of, in order to improve their bottom line. While a United States Air Force (USAF) military officer, he saved taxpayers $3.6 billion dollars by leading his team to assess and cancel a major acquisition program. Paul had a two-year break in service and worked as a financial analyst for Mobil Oil Company in Houston and Beaumont, Texas.

After 20 years in the USAF, including 12 consecutive years in the Pentagon and a year as a Capitol Hill Fellow, working for a member of Congress in the United States House of Representatives, Paul retired in the rank of lieutenant colonel. After leaving the military, Paul started his motivational speaking company; is the author of the book, *Living on Higher Ground;* delivers business coaching; expense reduction consulting; and is host of The Wealthy Speaker Talk Radio Show. Paul shares his voyage from abject poverty to his vision for success. www.paullawrencevann.com

My Vision

Our family has been in the same church for roughly 120 years. During my senior year of high school, I became sick. There was a communicable illness going around. I went with my mom and my sister to visit my sister's friend in the hospital, and I became ill, was admitted to the hospital, and stayed for an entire week. When I entered the hospital, I was 163 pounds; when I departed, I had lost 20 pounds.

On the second day of hospitalization, I reached into the drawer next to my bed, and there was a Bible. I read the Bible from beginning to end. The Spirit began ministering unto me; and at the time, I was trying to decide on which college to attend and what I was going to major in. I can hear the quiet voice state, "You're going to attend Shaw University and major in business."

That's not all, the quiet voice also directed me to rededicate my life to Christ and get baptized in church. I did everything requested of me and make no mistake about it – my faith and my spirit helped propel me — to see the vision that I could not see for myself.

It took the week of Thanksgiving 1975 for me to receive that vision and I applied to attend Shaw University and this was the beginning of my path to success. That's how things got started for me.

My Voyage

I'll share with you how my vision and purpose came about in my life. For me, I want to go back a little bit in my history to the age of 12. I was one of nine children growing up in rural North Carolina – Henderson, North Carolina, to be exact. My parents were both factory workers. I was the oldest son in a family of nine children.

At the age of 12, my parents put me to work in their community grocery store. Mind you, they were factory workers, but they didn't make a lot of money. Financially, it was very difficult for them to take care of us.

For me, that was really the pivotal point of my life when I found myself saying, "Poverty doesn't agree with me." I had a bigger vision. One of the blessings I had as a child was the blessings and visions of a dreamer. I had dreams that at some point in the future became reality. Throughout the course of my youth, I always dreamed about flying. At the time, I couldn't put it together. I guess later on in life, those dreams were about me serving in the Air Force.

One night, my aunt Karolyn was keeping my older sister and I while my parents went to a Christmas party, she woke me up and said, "You're having a nightmare. What were you dreaming about?"

I said, "Mom and Dad were in a car accident tonight." Later on that night the sheriff dropped them off at home. They had been in a car accident. I realized I had a special gift that to this day reveals things to me before they happen.

Fast forward, I am the first child in the family of nine to earn a high school diploma. After me, all my other brothers and sisters have graduated. Neither of my parents graduated from high school nor my grandparents before them. I was the very first one. Education is what I saw as my path to get out of poverty.

I didn't have any money to attend college, but I knew I wanted to go to college. I received about $300 from my graduation gifts, and then I had a summer job working at the recreation department in my hometown in Henderson, North Carolina. As a result of this, I started applying for grants, because my parents just didn't have any money to give me. At the age of 16, I started writing grants for myself. This was coming on the heels of my high school guidance counselor telling me I didn't have what it took to be a successful college student.

I graduated from Vance Senior High and attended Shaw University for four years. I was a distinguished graduate of AFROTC as well as an honor graduate, after earning a Bachelor's degree in business. I had worked for my parents since I was 12 thus I majored in business and minored in accounting. This was the path and the vision for me to come out of poverty.

I was commissioned a second lieutenant in the United States Air Force on the day that I graduated from Shaw University. That really turned my life around. Education was the path. It was the vision for me to turn everything around.

My academic success inspired my younger brothers and sisters. They followed in my footsteps and got an education as well. That's really what got me on my path to success, getting that education and then having a vision for more than just poverty. I did not appreciate the fact we were in poverty. I thought, "There's got to be a way to get out of this." It came through education.

The Value of Lessons Learned

The things I was experiencing were things my family had never experienced before. For example, no one before had attended college in my immediate family. That was a totally new experience.

The second thing was attending the USAF basic training camp. I attended basic training in Dover, Delaware for six weeks. I did not know what that experience would be like. I left my summer job at UPS; I worked for them for 3-1/2 years. I had no concept or idea that I would come back and join the two-year Air Force ROTC program. I was able to overcome the unknowns. I had to learn how to march. We'd get up at 5:00 in the morning, run a mile-and-a-half, do exercise, clean our room, and have white glove inspections every single day. That was really challenging for me.

Then I went into the Air Force about six months after the graduation. I went on active duty. It was a new culture. I had to learn the different military terms to use. I went into the acquisition field. I was working with three-and-half billion dollar acquisition programs, communications systems, and that's what got me started doing what I do today, expense reduction. I had to make the right decisions for my team of analysts to save taxpayers' money, because the contractor wasn't capable of delivering the USAF contract within budget and on schedule. That was a tough challenge because I reported directly to a no nonsense two-star general.

The other thing I was faced with was my parents' health that was on the decline due to all of the factory work they had performed for a tobacco company for 28 and 27 years respectively. I found myself periodically flying back and forth from Dayton, Ohio, where I was stationed, to Henderson, North Carolina. That became a big challenge for me to overcome. Wanting to know one's parents are doing well and being away from them was really the greatest challenge for me.

Other challenges that I ran into were some personal health problems; I came down with Lyme disease while assigned to the Pentagon. I almost lost my memory. I was able to overcome it, but it took me almost a year to recover.

I saw that I was being given a second chance; and as a result, I was able to make that recovery, regain my full health, and return to being productive. It was almost like I was starting all over.

I started realizing that some events in my life represented a new day for me. My life was starting all over because I was given another chance. I started taking advantage of those opportunities. It inspired me and motivated me to live fully because we really don't know when the next life challenge is going to happen.

I started my business, Wealth Building Academy as a motivational speaker. Then it transitioned to writing my first book, *Living On Higher Ground*. I started conducting life coaching and business success coaching. Ultimately, I received certification as a diversity trainer and delivered diversity and inclusion training for Fortune 500 companies, which was a major service deliverable for me.

Words of Wisdom and Vision

When it comes to expense reduction consulting and how to help an organization's bottom line, most small to mid-size companies actually have savings in their company. They don't even have to go out and sign new clients because, when they bring me in with my expertise to take a look at their financial books, I will review their contracts and be able to show them where they have savings. They probably have them, but people who work for them are too busy to identify savings and or don't know where to start.

I can also analyze different functional areas, such as real estate and look at the contracts associated with them. That's not all! I can review office supply contracts, communication expenses or company utilities. There are different aspects and areas to review and conduct an audit on corporate contracts. I've been certified to perform expense reduction analysis and identify areas in which a company doesn't realize they are losing money in.

Then, another area that I can analyze for a company is unclaimed funds they happen to have because small to mid-size businesses purchase, procure or acquire other companies. However, they don't have the same people looking at the full spectrum of their books. The financial books are very important. I can look at them and am able to identify savings for a company. The beauty of it is, I come in free of charge to perform expense reduction. After identifying savings for a company, I receive a percentage of the savings. There's no upfront cost involved whatsoever. That's another aspect I offer my clients.

Another area I look at includes how a company's staffing and personnel is structured. It's very important in terms of how personnel staffing is structured by a company, the head count is crucial and how they're utilized to maximize human potential. Are employees properly staffed? If they're not properly staffed, do they have the expertise to actually do the work they're assigned to perform?

Organizations are very dynamic. They bring in new people all the time, but sometimes the people at the top don't necessarily look at all the moving parts. I bring all the moving parts together for leadership, and I'm able to show them how their organization should work.

Those are just some of the areas. Contract management, which I mentioned before, reviewing the bill paying services that are taking place, and then different ongoing invoices, as well as staff training. If companies and organizations start to take a closer look at what is actually taking place, they can improve their bottom line without obtaining new clients. They already have savings, but they just don't have anyone who can actually focus on that. That's where I come in as a certified expense reduction consultant.

13. Become Excellent
Luis Vicente Garcia

Luis Vicente García is an international speaker, best-selling author, and a Certified Business Performance Coach who has studied how motivation and attitude influence the success of businesses. Married for 22 years with two sons, Luis has spoken to and trained thousands of people in different countries, has authored seven books, writes internationally syndicated columns and is the author of *Mindset Revolution* (CD Program).

An Economist with an MBA, he also holds master's degrees in Service Enterprise; Managerial Leadership; and Strategic Organizational Leadership, being a firm believer in continuing education. He is a member of Bestselling Authors International, The National Academy of Best-selling Authors and The Academy of Experts, Writers and Speakers.

His books include *Motivando al Futuro Franquiciado*; *101 Preguntas y Respuestas sobre las Franquicias*; and has co-authored *The Ultimate Success Guide*; *Dare to Succeed*; *Ready, Aim, Influence!*; *SuccessOnomics*; and *Ready, Aim, Inspire!* www.luisvicentegarcia.com

My Vision

I try to constantly motivate and inspire people all around me. It is - besides my consulting, coaching and speaking practice - a full time job. It's not easy, but very rewarding. Sometimes people ask me, "How do you get that inspiration? How do you get that energy?" I make a joke and say, "I have these energy pills — which you can buy only if you accept the responsibility." Then they ask me, "Where did you get those energy pills?" I say, "Inside You." There's nobody better to motivate ourselves than ourselves. There's nobody better to inspire us than ourselves, because when you are motivated and inspired, you can do wonderful things. I call my energy pills my Vitamin C; and the C is for Creativity, Commitment and Compromise.

First of all, you start by motivating others. Second, you continue by inspiring others. I have studied people who have been very successful, and there's something very interesting to me. *I have never found a successful person who is not positive!* Everybody who is successful is a positive person. If you combine motivation with your own positive attitude and with your own way of inspiring other people, just imagine what we could do together; only if everybody thought that way.

The way I find my personal style to inspire others is by showing what I do constantly and continuously, and by helping people sometimes without being paid for it. I believe people have the right to be better every single day, every single time.

I get invited to speak at Universities, and I get in touch with a lot of students. Sometimes you'll really look at them and you can see they know who they are, what they want to accomplish, and who are very interested in what you're saying. They are taking notes very quickly, looking at you and thinking new ideas while you are speaking. In that way, you feel that you are getting connections with them: they want to learn, to improve, to be successful.

For many people, success is many different things. For me, success is *'to create the path that will lead you to where you want to go and doing it successfully.'* There's a story about a group of hikers who were to climb Mount Everest. The usual ritual is that you meet beforehand with Buddhist monks. Usually they will come out of there and probably not understand what the monk said because usually he would have said something profound, like *"Your goal is to keep yourself on the road."* Most of us never understand that simple idea. The goal is not only to reach the top of Mount Everest; although it is. The real goal is to go up, stay on course; and if your journey is successful, you will come down safely, and that's the important journey. And it is the same for climbing Mount Everest as it is from our day to day business and personal lives.

We all go through different journeys throughout our lives. To be successful, we have to go through each different journey time and time again, and become successful doing it. Our next journey will be based on what we accomplish in this one and you start by being positive.

My Voyage

My journey started in Caracas, Venezuela, where I was born.

And as the journey transformed into my voyage, it's been a very interesting process. I graduated in 1984 and I finished my MBA by 1986. Since then, I've committed to my education: seminars, courses, workshops, and getting three additional Master's Degrees. The reason — because we all have to keep learning to become excellent.

For me, when everybody starts working to just enter into a company, you never know what's going to happen. You never know if you're going to be there for 40 years or two years, or for just a couple of days. Ten, 15, 20 years ago, it was customary for people to go and enter a company and probably work there forever or probably change jobs only twice in their whole career. Today, people are looking for jobs that are new and challenging. It is now customary to see résumés where people in their late 20s already have three or four jobs because they want a job that is a challenge. They will not do a regular job. They will not do regular stuff, because it's not the rule anymore.

We have to be creative. For me, this is something that since the beginning you have to learn. It's all the learning, adapting and accepting the information and understanding the different ways of people who manage teams and people who become leaders. By then, you have to start building your own style of management, your own style of leadership, and in a way that it develops yourself.

At a certain point, probably about five years ago, I said to my wife, "I want to do something different." I didn't know what it was at that time. I went to my boss and said that I was going to resign. He asked, "Why?" My answer was, "Because I wanted to do something different." And then he said, "Well, when you figure out what it is, talk to me again."

It took me a year, before I went back to him. We finally agreed I was going to leave the company. But then other events happened. Sometimes you have certain dreams beforehand; and at that time, I was offered the position of CFO at a multinational company. Of course, coming from a financial background, I went ahead and accepted it.

However, after a while something again was talking to me in the back of my head and it kept saying, "It's time for you to do something different." It took me probably a year to figure it out.

What I do now is help and guide people and organizations; I help people grow and prosper in different ways. I help young students become leaders. I help organizations grow and perform better and all because it's doable. You can do whatever you set out to do if your mind, your body, your thoughts, and your family are all together, behind you and supporting you.

I finally understood my purpose in November 2012. I resigned the CFO position, and I embarked on a journey as we were talking about. My journey was to define what to do. Today I can tell you I really enjoy what I'm doing. I'm a business coach, a performance consultant, a motivator and I love doing it. I'm a speaker; I usually speak about leadership and success, and always about positive attitude and personal motivation.

Early in 2014, I was invited to a University, and they asked me to give a speech called "Yes, you can do it!" That was the whole subject of my conference – "Yes, you can do it!" It doesn't matter where you are or where you come from; it doesn't matter what you can do. What really matters is that you think you can do what you are set to do.

Now I also have the opportunity to write. I have published two books of my own, have co-authored five books, and I write several blogs and columns. That's the way for me to help people; to let them know that there are new ideas out there.

There are new possibilities for you to become an entrepreneur. You can enter whatever area or development you want to pursue. By continuing your education, you start learning new ways to do the same thing but in a different manner or in a different form. You start getting those new ideas that will push you away from where you are today and get you closer to where you want to go.

There's something very important – you have to understand where you are today. If you do not do that, it doesn't matter which road you take because it will never take you anywhere. *You have to define where you are and you have to define where you want to go.* Then, you need to understand that the most important thing is how you're going to get there. It all ties together because you have to understand what you want to do, and then start doing it.

The Value of Lessons Learned

When people say, "You're an economist. You worked in finance for 25 years, and now you take care of people. What happened? When did something happen?"

I was giving a conference several months ago and I put it this way – "Companies report numbers, but then the numbers are produced by people. If the people are well motivated and they have a positive environment in which they work, the results are going to be incredible. If on the contrary, they are not motivated, they don't have a good leader, they don't have a good manager, or the environment they work in is a very negative one, you will not get the results you want."

Either your people are very well managed or they are not. They are placed in a very good and positive situation or they are not, and you see the results. I am working with different clients right now where if there's a positive environment, ideas are generated, and you can see the commitment that everybody has, the influence that all the different managers start having on each other, and the growth potential they find out.

I noticed that it is the people who generate the results for the different companies. Of course, everybody is just looking for the bottom line or the revenues or their indexes and how well they compared to last month, last year, to your competitors, etc. But when you see that these companies work in different ways, that you are able to really express yourself in the way a company that wants to grow and wants to prosper is expecting you to express yourself, then you have infinite possibilities.

Just look at the passing years – now we see companies that were not even thought about. Apple had an article earlier last year talking about how many apps they had produced and how many people were already in the apps industry. It didn't even exist five years ago. Just by creating a product that needed some apps, they created a new industry that generated new jobs that are now generating apps for these new phones, tablets and eventually the computers that will be out in the market.

The market has changed, and the people's needs have changed.

We have managers and leaders; and those people who are owners of companies, they just need to figure out a way to understand how to motivate the personnel they have working for them, how to allow ideas to flow. When you see the history in different areas – the Big Mac, for example, was created by a franchisee, not by McDonald's Corporation. And you have Coca Cola products that have different flavors in different parts of the world that you will not find in other countries. You start seeing the different possibilities your own company and your team have if they work in the right direction.

Words of Wisdom and Vision

I talk about excellence. I usually tell people, "You have to become excellent, not be average." But becoming excellent, is not only an ability... it's a lot of work. We may find every single time, every single day, every single month, there's a lot of work that goes into that.

There's something very critical we can do, and that is to find out where you are today. Look at it deeply. Not do it simply just because you wanted to say, "Okay, I did it." Really sit down; think where you are and think where you want to go. Then you will need to tie the two dots – one is here, the other one is in the future, and then set your blueprint in order to get there.

The goal is not what you want to reach – your goal is to have a safe journey and enjoy the voyage while doing it. My recommendation for everybody is to understand where you are today, where you want to go, and then draw the line which will be the trip you're going to take from here to there, and start developing right away.

Never waste your time. Do it right now. Never waste a single second that you can use for learning. I'm a firm believer of continuous learning because that's the only way we will improve constantly. That's the only way we will be better people and better professionals. Once you do it, you will see how your journey will transform itself into the Voyage to your Vision.

14. Express Yourself
Viki Winterton

Viki Winterton founded an eight-figure ad agency in her mid-20s, and created 25 years of worldwide coaching success with Fortune 100 companies and entrepreneurs.

Viki has also created two global coaching and writing networks, broadcast shows, three award-winning magazines, The Bestselling Authors International Organization, EIPPY Book Awards and Expert Insights Publishing—home of best-selling books, where visionaries and those on the rise come together to create immediate impact!

Viki has the proven formula you need to enhance your presence, empower your vision, and expand your influence for success. www.ExpertInsightsPublishing.com

My Vision

I have been an entrepreneur since I started a neighborhood newspaper when I was eight-years-old. I came by it naturally. My father was a barnstormer, and then a glider pilot in the Air Force. His sense of adventure was one of the many things I adored about him and soon emulated.

I developed a national ad agency when I was in my mid-20s, and was acquired three years later. My clients, many Fortune 100 companies, requested my services in the area of change management and process reengineering with their teams. This became a great career that took me all over the globe for over 25 years.

Coaching executives and teams fueled a desire to give back to my fellow coaches and entrepreneurs. It started with one community where coaches could find everything they needed, and quickly parlayed into two global communities, three magazines, broadcast venues, live events and Expert Insights Publishing, producing over 450 best-selling authors.

My Voyage

When I was working in advertising, big clients brought more big clients through referrals. That's how we grew to eight-figures in just three years. Back then, that really was a lot of money.

When I was coaching Fortune 100 companies, more top corporations would request my services as a result of project success stories. This created my dream career, tremendous income, and world travel for over a quarter of a century.

I wanted to bring this success formula to other coaches and entrepreneurs through our communities. Those communities soon spawned projects, vehicles, and businesses to bring our coaches and entrepreneurs together with visionaries and celebrities to create immediate impact and expert recognition.

The possibilities continue to unfold. However, it was just in the last few years that I discovered the most powerful vehicle of all—your book!

The Value of Lessons Learned

When I was first approached to do a book a few years ago, I was simply not ready. It seemed so complicated, and indeed it can be.

I understand that many may feel the same way I did. There's a lot to it, such as:

· You have to have a concept, and then write the book.

· You must have a catchy title and subtitle.

· You need to design the cover to attract readers.

· You should get a celebrity to write the foreword.

· You need to get experts to endorse your book.

· You have to have your book professionally edited.

· You need to evaluate publishing strategies.

· You need to decide if you should find an agent or a publisher.

· You need to decide if you should go the traditional publishing route, or self-publish.

- You need to get promotional support for your book from joint venture partners and networks.
- You need to establish a PR plan and promotional strategy.
- On release, you need to actively promote your book.
- Traditional publishing can take 18 months to three years, if you are accepted.

You can hire people to help you, but pros are expensive all along the way. I spoke with a NY Times best-selling author recently who spent over $15,000 on her book's initial editing alone.

When I was first asked to participate in a book, it scared me and I turned away. I set up an editorial review board and talked the publisher into running a content submission contest so that one of our entrepreneurs would win the opportunity based on the merit of their writing. We did this three times for different books featuring celebrities as co-authors. I saw how much our new book authors benefited. It was amazing how it propelled their businesses and raised their recognition as experts.

What has becoming an author and publisher done for me?

In one word: Visibility. It opened new doors to media and interviews that would never have been possible before. It also paved the way for amazing joint venture partners, and bigger and more profitable projects and events than I had ever dreamed of.

I also get to work and become friends with some of the coolest people in the world and discover their success secrets. We have expanded our community memberships and developed brand new bigger and better programs.

Some of our contributing authors have used the books as required materials for their corporate clients throughout the world; some have used their books to close huge coaching and consulting contracts.

I was warned, "You're not going to make money selling books. You're going to make money by *having* a book and using it to close more deals." That has been my experience—an experience far exceeding my goals and my vision!

We also donate the Amazon proceeds from the launch of each of our books to a deserving charity. It has been wonderful and rewarding to give back to the world in such a big way. In the last year, over 300 of our first-time best-selling co-authors have joined us in experiencing and celebrating that joy and success at our annual VIP awards live event!

Words of Wisdom and Vision

We wanted to figure out a process where we could help people become authors easily so they're not scared off like I initially was by the time, the energy, the effort, or the money. So here is our success formula:

1. *We put together a compilation book series*—a collaborative book, much like *Chicken Soup for the Soul*, where we interview you for your best ideas so readers can use them to improve their lives and get inspired. Your personal chapter and professional story can inspire others to get involved and can make a

difference in their lives and the lives of people around the globe. When they get this valuable information from you out of a published book, they imagine what they would get if they paid for your services.

2. *Essential elements: A catchy title and subtitle are critical, as is a cover that will attract the attention of readers and the media.* The book design has to be of superb professional quality. We want the book's quality to be absolutely spectacular. If we're going to put our name on it, it's got to be great. We've developed a proven formula with this best-selling series.

3. *Key Tip: Get the word out early about your forthcoming book!* Put it on your website, and in your bio! We do this for you with your name and photo on the cover. We post your forthcoming book on your book's Facebook and Wordpress pages and push the announcement out to the web. A professional press release from our world-renowned publicist goes out across the globe. We will prepare the entire book launch campaign. We promote massively! This is a truly collaborative event. We rally our professional connections, global communities, and joint venture partners to get the word out.

4. *Align with celebrities.* After over 1,300 personal interviews with visionaries and experts worldwide over the last few years, we have built special relationships to attract top-of-mind household name authorities to join us as book contributors and promoters and we share that advantage with you.

When you do what you love, and you do it in the company of visionaries and household names, you become an instant expert in your field.

15. Discover Your "Why"
Divya Parekh

Divya Parekh, CEO of The DP Group, eVirtual Roundtable Team Leader, and Career Community Leader for ICA has over 25 years of rich and varied experience as a university associate professor, scientist, biotechnology professional and global leadership wellness coach. Through inspired leadership, focused and tailored plans, she helps executives, professionals, coaches and youth embrace their inner confidence and endeavor for continual enrichment to achieve desired potential and success. She helps coaches, trainers and service providers develop customized information products for their clients. Divya's enormous love of people, fierce passion for coaching, commitment to building leaders and unbridled desire to change the world for the better has led to the establishment of The 1/1/1 Leader Project and launch of Podcast Show 'Careers Cast.'

She has been recognized as 'VIP of The 2013 Year' by Worldwide Who's Who for showing dedication, leadership and excellence in leadership coaching. She has also been recognized by NAPW as a 'VIP Woman of the 2014 Year' for outstanding leadership and commitment in coaching. She will be featured in Women of Distinction in 2015, a magazine division of the National Association of Distinguished Professionals. Divya has

been seen in press: BBC.com, CBS News, Haeretz.com, IGN, Daily Mirror, Daily News NY, Reuters, Slate.com, The Independent, TooFab, USA Today.
www.divyaparekh.com/111-leader-project/

My Vision

Although, passion is extremely important, you cannot build your life, business or organization on passion alone. Passion needs to be applied towards the dynamic purpose, and you need a process that will foster your passionate purpose towards success.

Purpose – To create the wealth of well-being for myself, others and us.

Purpose is the grit, the 'WHY' that galvanizes your passion and allows you to make a difference. Passion is the energy in your brilliance, is what you love to do and what makes you come alive. Vision is the junction where passion and purpose come together to create your pulsing dream/goal that you want for your life. Mission is the 'How' – the action plan to translate vision into reality to be the "you" you want to be.

I would like to share a short story. Once upon a time, a group of 60 people were attending a team-building workshop. The facilitator gave every participant a ball and asked him or her to write his or her name on it. All the balls were collected and placed in a container in another room.

The participants were guided to that room and asked to find the ball with their name written on it within 7 minutes. The majority of the participants dove into the container to find the ball with their name, paying no heed to their own or others' safety. As you can imagine, there was utter chaos and nobody could find their own ball.

Next, the facilitator asked each participant to randomly get a ball and give it to the person whose name was written on it. Within minutes, all the balls were in the hands of rightful owners.

The facilitator shares the purpose of the exercise. Most of us are looking for happiness and a sense of well-being everywhere, not knowing where to find it. What we do not realize is that our happiness and well-being is directly co-related to the happiness and well-being of other people. Kindness towards yourself contributes to your well-being. When you are kind to others, everyone, including you, experiences the wealth of well-being.

I believe that a shift in human consciousness is imminent where all of us can thrive together. Let's envision you as an inspired gardner. Like a great gardner, you know the science of needing your inner confidence to garden (thrive) and nurture the seeds (yourself, family, friends and community) each day so that the seeds (you and all) have a breakthrough, growth and unfolding into the best plant (you and all) that the seeds can be. Different elements like water, sunshine, shade, soil, nutrients and above all love of the gardner are needed to grow a beautiful garden.

The gardner knows that a balanced and cohesive organization of body, mind, feelings, intellect and connection to the community is needed for the well-being of an individual, family, community and planet.

The passion, that lights the fire in your belly, wakes you in the morning and relationship to the vision keeps you moving towards your goals. Just as a gardener is eager to see the unfolding of buds, you are ready to cherish the day you have in your hands. Although challenges, controversy, conflict, wins, concurrence, harmony will come your way, you, the gardener, learns, adapts and grows while experiencing the ever-evolving life. You, the gardener, know how to thrive using love, patience, kindness, equanimity and gratitude to sow the seeds (positive), weed the weeds (negative) while creating a harmony with the environmental elements. The smile is never too far from your lips or eyes. Your mindful energy makes you come alive, directs you to experience joy in anticipation of an emerging plant that grows and blooms in its natural splendor. Nothing changes and yet everything changes. This results in shifting the course of your life while influencing those who come in contact with you positively.

Let's expand the envisioning. Your energy draws the positive forces like a magnet. Because you are content, you want to share your joy and help others. As you help others, bonds of kindness become the glue of connections. Your home becomes a haven, your family where everyone belongs and wants to be a part of. As the joy spills over, consequentially you reach out to your friends, neighbors, and strangers. The connection of love and kindness begins with you and keeps zooming out. The gardening begins with a genuine 'me' merging into an enormous 'we' — leading to inspired leadership where freedom and love of learning fosters individual and collective growth.

Leadership wellness coaching is my passion because it enables me to be a gardener in true sense and experience the joy of seeing the dramatic shifts people make towards accruing and sharing the wealth of well-being. It could be the unfolding of a bud (person finding the courage to step into their awesome being that they are), creating space for new plants by weeding (generating confidence by releasing their emotional fears) or a tree you planted giving shade and home to birds (a leader discovering and following his purpose of helping others achieve what they want).

Mission – Wealth of well-being grows tenfold with courage of acceptance, kindness, mindfulness, grace and love in your heart. The 1/1/1 Leader Project movement and signature program starts out with developing an independent leader 'me,' bridging the connection with the other, be it friend, family or a fellow being by a smile followed through by building 'we' which are interdependent connections of independent 'MEs' (ME when flipped becomes WE) through kindness. "**Individually**, we are one **drop**. **Together**, we are an **ocean**." - Ryunosuke Satoro

My Voyage

My life has included successes and setbacks. At times, everything seemed to work; and at times, everything seemed off-kilter. It so happened that sometimes the personal development tools in my tool kit did not work. One of the biggest challenges has been to put myself first before work, family or friends. The other has been to acknowledge the truth about my ability to perform above par despite excruciating pain in my back and neck. In the pursuit of getting things done at all costs, I kept on pushing myself. During such times, the purpose fueled the embers of underlying passion to do whatever it takes to keep on marching towards the vision. I got caught in the cycle of paying some attention to my well-being, get a little better and drive myself farther. I had mistakenly thought I was in control, but I realized that the body was in charge. From there on began the quest of finding what stopped me, what is it that stops my friends and clients to make the complete shift from where we want to be. Coaching, meditation, nature, relationships and science soon became my allies.

As the science of the unconscious mind became the basis of coaching, the gap between knowing and doing amalgamated to become a way of life. Outcomes are driven by behaviors and habits, which in turn are driven by feelings/emotions. At the bottom of the feelings, are our thoughts and beliefs. Thus, our thinking drives our actions, behaviors and decisions affecting our well-being, optimal performance and results positively or negatively. The maxim 'Know thyself' revealed that my belief about my role in society led to an exaggerated sense of conscious responsibility. The pain became a blessing in disguise. When you are true to yourself and your core values, mindfulness aligns with environment and honors efforts, process and intentions, not just the results.

On one hand, mindfulness nurtures non-judgment, acceptance, grace and love. On the other hand, it develops inner confidence, positivity and courage born out of emotional freedom to nurture the seeds of opportunities in times of adversity. Science has shown that positive emotions expand your attention and outlook for a brief period as well as widen your perspectives and open you to new possibilities that did not exist before. This in turn leads you to develop personal cognitive (e.g. mindfulness), psychological (emotional dexterity), social (healthy relationships) and physical (e.g. greater ability to fight viruses) resources. It is to your advantage to integrate mindfulness and positivity in daily life.

The Value of Lessons Learned

We have made great strides in science and human consciousness evolution. The foundation of our purpose/vision/mission has been laid by our culture, environment and society. Skills, commitment, flexibility, fortitude, and positive thinking have become the tools to make our visions a reality and help us live a purposeful life. As a society, we want to flourish. Yet it is a reality – that our society is entangled in the web of needs, survival and instantaneous gratification. This leads to struggles with physical, mental and intellect woes, the roots of which are embedded in living lives without vision, passion and purpose. A life without a purpose makes you feel that you have toiled hard for decades and decades doing something that is not expressing you and dragging you down. You may ask why others have achieved unprecedented success while you, although equally matched, are not there yet. The truth is that wealth of well-being runs dry at some point because it is dependent on external factors. The truth is that when you tune into your purpose, it connects with your passion to create a vision of a cohesive way of being, intelligent decisions, connection with others and a mission of thriving.

It is not enough to define the situation/problem, it is important to study it inside out, finding out the "WHY" – the root cause, what you are working towards and how to get there, knowing that the 'whole is greater than the sum of its parts' (Aristotle). As you continuously evolve, rewire and create new neural circuits, you have learned that like good software, you require periodic upgrades to become the person you want to become.

The learnings and experiences led to an evolving 'The 1/1/1 Leader Project movement and signature program' that influences your unconscious mind to create and develop new beliefs, actions, behaviors, habits and benevolent decisions. This is turn makes you self-reliant, enabling you to succeed as you derive solutions from within, empowering others to become independent and build interdependent relationships to serve 'US.'

If you choose to, the following seven steps can help you create your own blueprint of well-being based on the foundation of purpose, passion and vision.

Key #1: Discover your 'POWERED BY ME "WHY"

You have to dive deeper than your life story, your experiences and issues to know yourself. As you discover your perspective on life, values, flaws, and strengths, you will discover true power that embraces 'YOU' with warts and all. When you are accepting of yourself, you will be accepting of others and ready to step into your GANDHI moments. Once you know yourself reasonably well, ask the following questions to unveil your purpose:

What is your "WHY" – your meaningful purpose that is powered by you and none other? To ensure that your purpose will stand the test of time ask-

- Does your purpose fit with your perspective of life, align with your values and what you stand for? If not, does your perspective of life need to be reevaluated?

- Usually, purpose is something that you are passionate about. Does your purpose strike an emotional resonance within you?
- Does your purpose expand beyond you and include the well-being of others?
- Know that you may be defining, redefining and refining your purpose as you continue to evolve and grow.

Key#2: Create, connect and integrate your vision in your life.

Once you know your purpose and passion, envision what your desired outcome looks like.

- Step into the authentic 'YOU.'
- Synergize with your relations (friends, family and community) to visualize how you, your loved ones, what you stand for, your values and contributions will come together as you realize your vision.
- Make a vision board of what you have envisioned with the help of your relations, inspirational quotes, stories and pictures. Keep it front and center so that you and your relations connect with and integrate your vision in daily life.
- Live and leave your legacy day after day.

Key#3: Cultivating creativity, Emotional intelligence, mindfulness and competency

The definitions pertinent to our discussion are given below:

Creativity is unrestricted flow of ideas resulting in simple games invented by children, development of new products, problem-solving traits, concrete manifestation of artist's vision and many others.

"Emotional intelligence (EQ) is the ability to perceive emotions, to access and generate emotions so as to assist thought, to understand emotions and emotional knowledge, and to reflectively regulate emotions so as to promote emotional and intellectual growth." Mayer & Salovey, 1997

Mindfulness is "the intentional accepting and non-judgmental focus of one's attention on the emotions, thoughts and sensations occurring in the present moment", which can be trained by meditational practices (Wikipedia)

Competency is the ability to do something successfully or efficiently.

Research has confirmed presence of four brainwave states that range from the high amplitude, low frequency delta (deep sleep) to the low amplitude, high frequency beta (active mental state). High amplitude, low frequency brainwaves promote free flow of ideas leading to meaningful, creative and productive mental activity. The following practices cultivate creativity, EQ and mindfulness and competency.

- Gain insight on mindset, beliefs, thoughts, feelings, and behavior cycle.
- Assess your present perspective with regards to body, mind, feelings, intellect and connection to the community. Let go of the excuses that hold you back.
- Leverage your strengths to keep the momentum flowing in small steps or big leaps.

- Increase self-awareness through mindful meditation, exercise, music, playing sports, arts, visualization, autogenic procedures, and neurolinguistic programming.
- Foster compassion and empathy towards others through acceptance with non-judgment.
- Practice active listening to your body, mind, feelings and intellect.
- Apply active listening to understand others' verbal and non-verbal communication.
- Action your way into creating new mindset.

Key #4: Lean into your fear with Emotional Intelligence and Mindfulness

Work through the fears by strengthening your mental muscles with EQ and mindfulness. Your fears focus primarily on loss of health, independence, life, rejection, and/or success. As Mark Twain aptly said, "Courage is resistance to fear, mastery of fear—not absence of fear. You can work through the fears to live your vision.

- Acknowledge your fears and emotions associated with it.
- Discover the cause of fears, whether external stressors or internal beliefs and mindsets.
- Face the fears and emotions with an open mind and empathy.
- Develop courage to create new and balanced mindsets.

Key#5: Help others with Emotional Intelligence and Mindfulness

Research has shown top-performing leaders have high EQ. Successful leaders with high EQ make better decisions and flourish socially. Employ EQ and mindfulness for others' benefits:

- Understand your actions can influence others' feelings and emotions.
- Manage your own feelings and emotions to produce constructive actions.
- Accept, learn from and work through the feedbacks and setbacks.
- Empathize with others through active listening.
- Show up as authentic 'YOU' everywhere.

Key #6: Become an Independent 'YOU'

You and I are aware of our life experiences filled with repeated mistakes and circling of wagons. This can be counteracted if you use a reflective and holistic approach that employs the discussed tools.

- Check in and challenge obstacles.
- Learn from experiences to bridge the gap between knowing and doing.
- Continue to acquire knowledge.
- Seek support.
- Celebrate wins with gratitude.

Key #7: Build a supportive and kind community

Begin with you and zoom out to your family, friends, neighbors, community, nation and planet. Help others to help themselves to become independent through love, kindness, grace, encouragement and inspiration. Lead to build a community of interdependent team members and serve for the greater good of 'us.'

The complex human body is an excellent example of a whole being. You can be compared to a system within the body that interacts with the other systems to keep the whole being healthy. You have specific functions, yet all the systems are interconnected and interdependent on one another to serve the whole being.

Words of Wisdom and Vision

Throughout our conversation, we have conversed about the paradigm of accumulating the wealth of well-being by paying attention to the body, mind, feelings and intellect as a whole. The paradigm can be optimally applied in life only if you are honest with yourself and believe that the secret factor of success is essentially 'YOU.' You have the power to lead the way to show up as your best in life and enable others to show up as their best in lives.

When someone says thank you, ask them to give a smile and do a kind act to another as a thank you. Live and leave your legacy day after day. As we part our ways for now, I leave you with a poem and an invitation to visit the website to sign the pledge of changing the world one connection at a time. Hope to connect with you!

The 1/1/1 Leader Project

Live life with purpose and meaning
For it nourishes your very being
Rather than complain and whine
Let's affirm and draw a line
Why wait until next election
For our leaders' selection
Let's make a connection
Give a gift of compassion
Initiate with a genuine smile
And dissolve that gaping mile
Set one personal goal
Achieve it even if you fall
To another, a kind word or deed
Build a connected community, seed by seed

16. From Problems to Possibilities
Dr. Richard Eley

"Let your mind see what your heart already knows."

2003 was the year...traveling to Salt Lake City to become Certified with Franklin Covey. Since that time, **Dr. Richard Eley** has gone through a metamorphous, while being accountable to his Coach, working as a Life Coach, a Leadership Coach, an Executive Coach. It has taken a while but now, "the Eagle" has landed on being a Small Business Coach.

Prior to this "metamorphous," there was almost 20 years in the arena as a therapist...working with people's "problems." NOW he has the opportunity to work with people's "potential."
www.richardeley.com

My Vision

"A vision begins in your heart and formulates in your mind."

As long as I can remember, my passion is and has been for people. Understand...I'm older than dirt. In fact, I am so old that I can remember when you used the phone to talk to people as we are today. It started as a teenager working at the YMCA in Michigan. I was offered to have my college paid for if I would promise to come back and work at the YMCA. I didn't follow that through, but that certainly was the beginning of my involvement working with people.

As a therapist for about 20 years working with people's problems, I became aware of a different process when I went to Salt Lake City, Utah in 2003, to become certified with Franklin Covey as a certified Franklin Covey Life Coach, beginning my journey towards helping people achieve their possibilities.

In the process of my developmental issues, I began to work on vision. From my point of view, I don't think vision is a one-step catchall that is there without some other foundational elements that have to be placed into the working process of developing a vision.

My Voyage

After being in Salt Lake City for a week of training, they said, "You are now a certified life coach with Franklin Covey."

I said, "That sounds good." I began to work with different coaches. I hired a coach, and we began coaching together. In our conversations, he said, "You know what, Doc? I don't think you're a life coach."

I said, "Wait a minute. I paid a lot of money to become a life coach."

He said, "In your conversations working with your clients, you sound more like a leadership coach."

I said, "That sounds pretty good. Can I charge more for that?"

We continued that process. As I continued working with individuals – managers, individuals just in every phase of life – I then started to work with small business owners. I said, "How about becoming an executive coach?" I started doing that and started charging more, and then I landed on the context of being a small business owner coach.

I didn't work strictly with small business owners – I worked with staff all through the business. I worked with them to help them develop a vision for their business, as I had developed a vision for my business.

I started out with what I felt was the most foundational part, and that was the development of my values. I think it's critical that everybody has values. In fact, I think it's so critical that I usually share with people a quote out of the bestseller, *The Leadership Challenge* (you probably are aware of this book).

The authors said this: "Shared values make an enormous difference to organizational and personal vitality. Research confirms that firms with strong corporate culture based on a foundation of shared value outperform other firms by a huge margin. Their revenue grew four times faster. Their rate of job creation was seven times higher. Their stock prices grew 12 times faster, and their profit performance was 750% higher."

I looked at that and said, "It's foundational then for me in my own personal life as well as my professional life that any small business that I work with understands that values are a foundation." After values comes a written manifesto. Write out how I am going to live my values out. These are habits, not goals. They are repeated actions that I do without exceptions as the embodiment of my deeply held personal values.

Then I learned another great process. After I had my values and manifesto, I needed a mission statement. There are a lot of small business owners, there are a lot of individuals who desire to have a vision, but have no idea where they're going or where they're headed. A mission statement is very critical in that process.

Working with a great coach, I came to my Mission Statement, which is, "*Inspiring People...Illuminating Their Passion*," and that focuses then in on my vision. Everything that I do centers on that Mission Statement.

The Value of Lessons Learned

Too often what happens in our life is that we don't have a purpose; we don't have a vision. Therefore, somebody else comes along, infiltrates my mind – which is the transformational system – changes my mind, changes that direction. But, if I am secure in knowing what my values are, my manifesto, my mission statement, other people can't come in and try to develop my life.

If I have no meaning to life, other people are going to give it to me. With this, I work with small business owners, individuals and families putting their criteria together. As children grow up, they grow up in a household that has values, a manifesto, and a vision statement, so when they're confronted with something, they line that up to those three major elements, and then they can say, "I can't do that because it doesn't line up with my life." This concept is the same for small business owners.

If I have that done, I can then change the world, because I know where I'm going, how I need to get there through my vision, and I can process it and put it into steps which are my goals. Then I have the criteria to make it a functional process in all that I do, all that I participate in, everything that I am going to do for the rest of my life.

Stephen Covey wrote a book, that you may be familiar with it, *The Seven Habits of Effective People.*

He describes very succinctly the process that I'm talking about. One of those 7 habits is, "Begin with the end in mind." There are several critical elements to those six words.

First, I have to "begin." That's the starting point.

Secondly is, "with the end." Where do you want to finish? Where do I want to be 5, 10, 15, 20 years from now?

I was working with a client just the other day, and we've been working together since about 2007-2008. He's a builder. He went through some real problems in 2008, but he's kept his head above water. This year he's back on target to make somewhere between three and five million dollars. He's still trying to process getting out of the rut back in 2008. He's doing that, keeping the end in mind, where he wants to finish.

We often overlook the Third part, and that is, "in mind." The mind is the place where any vision is created. For you to own the vision, it must be a creation of your mind, not someone else's.

Look at it this way...

> Values + Manifesto + Mission Statement + Goals + Transforming my mind = VISION

For almost 20 years, I was a therapist. Being a therapist and working with people, I found out over those 20 years that I was working with people's problems/struggles. I sometimes got into a rut, and most people ask, "What's a rut?" It's a grave with the ends kicked out. It became a mindset of just going through routine after routine after routine of trying to help people through their problems.

In 2003 when I went to Salt Lake City, I was really freed up at that point in time to see life as a whole different venue. Instead of working with people's problems, I began to work with their possibilities. There's a vast difference in working with people's problems and people's possibilities – not to say that there isn't a place for therapy and there isn't a place for clinical issues, but I was personally just freed up because now I have the freedom to work with people's possibilities.

People who are living in the here and now and wanting to get to their possibilities...I have a boat that can help get them from the Island of the Here and Now to the Island of Possibility. It just has been a great, freeing process. Freeing of my own heart, my own mind and my own transformation has allowed me to help individuals arrive to that same state of life.

For some of you who are fortunate enough to be traveling down a road of your own making that supports your dreams and goals, my hat is off to you. For the rest of you, I'd like for you to open your minds as you read the possibilities of redefining, redesigning, and ultimately re-loving your life.

It is my belief – and the belief of many personal and professional coaches – that the lives that we lead is more often a result of lack of planning than over-planning, or even having the wrong plan. The most successful people in the world are people who create and fulfill their own vision for their lives. They are the ones that have defined the meaning of their lives and are living on purpose.

Words of Wisdom and Vision

Vision begins in your heart and formulates in your mind. It becomes something imagined that you would like to make real for your life. Ideas turn into intentions and a desire to make something happen. A vision is the expression of your desires for a future that is better in some important way then what exists for you now.

Vision comes out of dreams. I ask of my clients that they take an hour once a week and just dream. Dreaming is a great freeing up exercise to give some direction and purpose, because it answers that question, "What if?"

It also helps me understand the identity of who I am and why I'm here. When I can solidify those thoughts, I have great appreciation for what's out there in life and what is available for me to accomplish. I can just keep going on and on. It's a great opportunity.

What I like to do as a coach is ask questions. Some questions that would help you towards making a Vision are:

- *What would make you happy?*
- *What would define a good job for you?*
- *What would good kids look like?*
- *What would you like to be the boss of?*
- *Why would you like to retire early?*
- *What would being rich mean to you?*

I encourage you to not make vision questions/statements vague and non-inspiring.

6 Dimensions of a Vision ~ There are 6 dimensions of a vision that will help lead you closer toward fulfillment:

- Imaginable
- Desirable
- Feasible
- Focused
- Flexible
- You must be able to communicate your vision.

There are many exercises designed to help people begin shaping their vision. Try the following exercise.

Pretend that it is your retirement. At that retirement party, you're going to have a family member, a fellow worker, a community leader, your boss, you're going to have somebody from maybe your church, or whatever it might be. They're going to say something really special about you. *What would you like them to say about you? How would you like to be remembered?* Now, you sit and write the article.

As I begin to dream, that begins to bring me back into the fold of beginning to work with what my vision might look like.

Here is a question to ask yourself: *Why Create a Vision?*

Every choice, big or small, we make in life has a cause and affect relation attached to it. Without the direction of a clear vision for guidance, we will likely fail in acquiring a life full of the abundance we want and hope for.

A clear vision of the future leads to satisfaction and a sense of meaning and purpose in life. The lack of a clear vision leads to settling for whatever happens; creating and staying true to a vision makes things happen.

Let Your Mind See What Your Heart Already Knows!

17. Achieve Through Education
Elizabeth Olagunju

Elizabeth Olagunju is a number one international best-selling author, and she's also an accomplished educator who has helped hundreds of people to step up in both their careers and personal lives.

In her experience as an elite coach, every committed client she has worked with has achieved results that far surpass their initial expectations.

She has helped move people in transition to achieve their goals and restore hope to those who thought there was nothing else to achieve in life. www.coaching4business4life.com

My Vision

My inspiration is my mother. My mother wanted to have an education so much, but was not able to because of her family background. She poured all that she had into my siblings and me so that we could be well educated. Unfortunately, she passed away suddenly before I finished getting my postgraduate degree.

That had been my driving force, to be able to impart onto others what my mother had imparted in me, and that was the gift of education, the gift of inspiration, the gift of encouragement. Moving people from one level of success to another, giving people hope and motivation and inspiration to let them know they can achieve. They can be what God, their creator, had made them to be; it was possible. There may be challenges, but they can get there.

I want to see as many people as I can coach in this life. If I can touch millions, I'll be glad and I'll be grateful to God. If I can touch millions and move them up to a higher level, to a higher contribution to this world, that would be my satisfaction.

My Voyage

I was the first person in my family to go to college. As I mentioned, that was my mother's dream, to make sure that I had what she did not have. I was the firstborn of seven children. In my culture, the first one has a lot of responsibility. I found it an honor, a privilege, and also a duty for me to get to the highest I can achieve in life and pull others with me to help them to also reach their level of success.

My mother sacrificed so much with my father to get me the education that I have. I received my first degree in Nigeria, my native country, and then I moved to America. Since I've been here, I got my Master's degree in education. I also have a MBA degree. I have worked for Fortune 500 companies. I have experiences and wisdom I want to share with others, because from my background of having nothing to having so much, it's a privilege, and I'd like others to have it, too.

The Value of Lessons Learned

During the voyage, the journey, the challenges are many, especially in terms of financial. Coming from the third world, as they used to call it, the developing world, my first degree I got through a scholarship from the government. Without the scholarship, I would not have been able to get my college degree.

When you have a scholarship, you don't have luxuries. I managed through financially, some days eating only once a day so that I could get my education and complete my degree. By the grace of God, I was able to get my first degree in the sciences, and I became an expert at entomology. I moved here to the US. I was also helped through a scholarship I got from PEO International Scholarships. This helped me to get through my postgraduate studies.

This makes having money a privilege for me, because I've come from having nothing to being able to have something. I've also seen that it's been through the help of other people, those who had opened their arms to help me that I've been able to get here. I would like to pay back and help as many as I can in this world.

My book, *Raising High-Achieving Kids: 7 Ways to Enhance Your Child's Future* is very close to my heart, because I poured all my experiences, all I have gone through as a mother and also as someone seeking to move higher in life. With my four children, I was still able to continue with my education and also get involved in their vocational world.

One of the seven ways in my book is positivity. Be a positive person. When you are a positive person, your child will see it and will also emulate you. Be inspiring to your child; know what is number one. Placing your priorities right. When your child sees that, they surely pay attention to you and whatever you say. Be positive to your children.

Also, let them know that we have control. There are many people who think that all the things that happen to them in this world are outside their control. No, no, no. You can control what is happening to you, because when you take responsibility for your life and what is happening to you, then you'll be able to achieve more.

Let them know that they can control what's happening to them, and they can determine what they want to do in life by being in control. Don't let others rule over them or let negativity control their life.

Number two is discipline. Children need to know that discipline is very important, especially self-discipline. When you know how to discipline yourself, then you'll be able to plan the different ways you want to succeed in life. So many successful people that I've talked to placed self-discipline as the number one thing that helped them to reach their goals in life. Start encouraging your children to have self-discipline, and also discipline them while they're young. Don't leave it to when they are older, because then it will be too late. We have to learn to discipline our children, and we have to start early.

Number three would be a positive attitude. Help them to develop a positive attitude while they are young. That will carry them a long way in life. They need to see that the cup is not always half empty. They always need to look at the positive things of whatever is happening to them in life, because there will be challenges in life. Teach your children to develop a positive attitude.

Number four: It's very important to also know what they're actually passionate about in life. What do they like to do in life? What is their passion? If they know it early in life, it will save them from a life of struggles of agony of deciding what matters, what they want to do, what do they not want to do. Some people go through a series of studies and even college and they still don't know what they want to do in life.

It's good to get your children to start defining what they are passionate about. Once they know what they are passionate about in life, they will never work in their life, because whatever they are doing they will enjoy it. They'll wake up every morning ready to go do whatever they want to do.

When they are passionate, they can have the number five attribute for a successful life, which is to be innovative. When you are passionate about something, you get creative. You have an innovative mind to want to make it better, because things will always be the same if nobody thinks that it could be done another way.

When your children know what they want to do in life, the sky is the limit for what can come out of that. The child will be innovative and will be able to leave a contribution to the world. With a positive attitude the child has developed, there will even be more possibilities to be achieved.

The sixth one is, you have to develop in your child the power of your words. The power of speaking positively to your child. When the child notices that in you, he or she will learn from you, and that will grow their ability to be positive and to have a very creative mind. All these things work together. One leads to another one.

Last but not least is confidence. You need to develop confidence in your child. How do you do that? Do that from the very beginning of life. It starts from the way you treat your child. It starts from the way you develop self-esteem in that child. From the self-esteem of a child in the home, that leads to having self-esteem at work and also in the community.

I found that what helped me most was I had my priorities right. I was able to determine what my path was and put first things first. When I placed taking care of my children as the center of my purpose, it helped me to make every other activity fall into their right places. I was able to bring these four children to this country, and also, by the grace of God, saw that they all got their education and their college degree, positioning them for their career in life right now.

What helped me to do that was because I put them first, in the center. Every other activity fell into the right places. I was able to encourage them, to inspire them, and was able to be a role model to them so that they could see that it is possible, and what they can achieve.

This is what I want to share with other parents, too. Parents need to be role models. Parents need to be encouraging to their children. Parents need to lift their children up instead of pulling them down. They always need to be there for them.

Words of Wisdom and Vision

If you're at the point in your life now that you're thinking should you get an education or not, whether you just finished high school and you're thinking if you should go to college, I would say it's a good question to ask, because there may be challenges. There may be a mother with children around wondering, "How will I take care of these children?"

I was in that situation too with my four children, and I was wondering, "How could I go for another degree with four children?" But I felt that if I stayed where I was, I would not move forward.

The first thing you want to ask yourself is with your high school education, how far will that take you? If you can think of how far it will take you, is that where you want to be forever in life? Can you gain more? I had thought of that. I know there are some people who do not even go to high school, and with a grade school education they've become rich. It is possible. But I have also found that for self-fulfillment and also for your self-esteem, even having a high school diploma will help you much, much more. Just a high school diploma.

I remember reading the story of Whoopi Goldberg. She did not go to high school until after she had become very famous. She could not go to a regular high school; she had to do it from home as an adult, and then she got her high school diploma, a GED. When I read the story, I was really amazed. This was somebody who had become famous, was a celebrity, and she felt it was necessary for her to get that GED.

You may be famous, you may become rich, but for your own self-fulfillment and even more self-confidence, it's always good to have that qualification. These days, things have been made so much easier, especially for mothers. You can do it online. There are so many opportunities to do one certification or the other online. You may even be able to get your high school diploma taking classes online. There are so many resources that you can find. You can check with your state or with any school or educational personnel around you.

I would highly encourage you to take a little step further. It never hurts. Everybody should always be learning. Never stop learning, because there is always something new to learn.

Voyage to Relationships

18. Make One Child Matter
Mike Fritz

What do you get when you mix a stand-up comedian with someone who has a master's degree in leadership and travels the world speaking to high school and college students? One of the most sought-after speakers in America! **Mike Fritz** has delivered over 1,500 paid talks, and is the author of the best-selling books, *Great Student Leaders Aren't Born, They're Made* and *Making Leadership F.U.N.* He has shared the stage with NFL quarterback and Super Bowl champion Joe Theismann; Glen Morshower, Aaron Pierce on the hit TV show *24* and also star of *Transformers*, and LA Clippers Assistant Coach, Kevin Eastman, just to name a few. His passion to change the world through bringing aid to needy children and inspiring the next generation is unmatched. www.mikefritz.net

Vision

The discovery of my vision has not a straight line. I don't know if you have figured that out, but visions often reveal themselves to us a little bit at a time until they completely crystallize for you.

I've worked with youth group organizations for over 10 years now, and I've always had a passion to see the next generation succeed. The first student organization I worked with, we had a student come to our group one night who looked like he was having a rough day. What I didn't know at the time was that night would change my life forever. A long story made short is he went home that night and attempted suicide. After his attempted suicide, the doctor told him he had 10 percent chance of being permanently paralyzed. That "small" percentage happened to be true, and he is now paralyzed from the waist down.

That moment I also realized the rest of my life was going to be given over to helping students in high school, college, and then what now has led me to my nonprofit that I work with, One Child Matters. One Child Matters is about providing a preemptive strike for kids who have no hope unless somebody steps in.

You know how you have those defining events in your life? That was one of those events that turned my head and made me say, "As long as I'm able, I'm going to give my life to the next generation." That's taken on three different aspects. Speaking to high school students, college students, and now into my nonprofit, One Child Matters. We are partnering with people all over the country and world to bring food, clothing, shelter, water, and education to kids in over 16 countries. We have over 40,000 children sponsored at this point. That's a snapshot of the journey of how I got to this place.

My Voyage

That situation single-handedly opened my eyes to the fact that students don't grow up in nice little boxes with picket fences. If we're really going to get involved in helping students, we're going to have to get involved in the junk of their lives, be willing to get our hands dirty, and enter their world.

As I said, the journey has been a little disjointed, but it's all come together in that my entire passion now is aimed at the next generation, at high school and college students, and now it's brought me into this as nonprofit, One Child Matters, of getting aid to kids all around the world.

As I looked at the next generation, I saw things that not only needed to change, but I thought I could be instrumental in changing. Whether it'd be this young man trying to commit suicide, or a young child without food, shelter, clothing or water. For example, I did a lot of intervention counseling with students, which was very, very hard, because you're meeting with these students day in and day out, and you are really seeking to bring aid, and then they go back into these homes that are not the best from a number of perspectives.

I can remember one young man who came in with his mom and was involved deeply in cutting. This student's life, at least to him, was so bad he resorted to one thing he could control – self-inflicted pain. Those are the challenges today that really fuel my mission when I feel like I'm not impacting the number of students I would like to.

All of us hit those days when it's like, "I don't really know if it's working" or doubt if we should keep going. It was those challenges day in and day out working with students and feeling like I wasn't getting anywhere, trying to say, "Why don't you try this to bring your life around?" and them not trying it, and watching them go further into despair. It was very challenging watching that because I knew what they could be and could do if they would make a different choice.

The Value of Lessons Learned

Many times I thought, "Am I even really having an impact of telling this next generation how to live differently?" Challenges often come up; but what has happened in those situations have now become my fuel to say, "I'm not going to give up," and has now turned into working to get these physical needs met all across the globe for kids who have no voice in their lives.

That's just a few of the challenges that really knocked me off guard and hit me hard. It's the moment of challenge when how serious you are about your vision is really determined.

The number one challenge that we see today in students is the issue of identity. This is not just a national issue but rather shows up around the globe. This is also a major issue when it comes to adults. The issue of identity deals with who you are, what defines you and what gives you worth. Today we see students (and adults for that matter) judging their worth based on comparing to others around them, what kind of job they have or how much money they make. However, identity has to do with who you are at your core and what makes you tick - note these peripheral issues.

This world tells them who they should be, whether it be a young woman looking at advertisements and falsely deciding what true beauty is and they pursue that form of beauty, or it can be guys thinking they've got to be a certain way to be this "socially accepted" man and so on. Or, it could even by parents trying to, in essence, live out their desires through their kids.

What ends up happening is we have kids undecided who they really are, and they don't even really know who they want to be. We have them giving up who they want to be and what they want to accomplish and their own vision for what everybody else thinks they want them to do. That's the greatest struggle we see in student culture today.

This, I really believe, is the core problem of why we're seeing a rise in suicide, self- destructive behavior, drug, alcohol, substance abuse, and cutting, just to name a few. So many of these things are hitting our young culture, even the massive trend of bullying from coast to coast. It really all comes back to this core issue of identity; our students are not being fueled and allowed to be who they truly are, embrace it, and allow it to flourish. Instead they're seeking to become what everybody else thinks they should be.

Even tailoring that to why I'm so passionate about One Child Matters and getting children sponsored is because when a child grows up without food, shelter, water, clothing, education — some of the essentials of life — they assume that that's just how it is – that's it's normal to grow up with very few options, with limited resources. Part of what our sponsors bring those kids is hope that now there's a greater calling for them and a greater mission for their life than what they've been exposed to, and we would like to expose them to more.

It's not just money. Many of these amazing international students want to be musicians, singers, writers, but they have no way to get there. When you ask what the greatest issue today is, I really believe it's this issue of who are they; are they are allowed to be that person, and are we helping them find that person rather than masking it with what we think they ought to be. We're not really giving them latitude to flourish in their own skin. That's what I'm seeing, not only coast to coast, but I've taken trips to Honduras and other countries around the world, and it's the same there.

Words of Wisdom and Vision

Here's what I often say to parents – a couple tips. Number one, help your child discover who they are; don't tell them who they are. The point is, your child is different than you. A lot of times we get this misnomer that because my child is made up of my DNA that they are like me. Now, they may have some similar looks and some similar desires because they've grown up in your home, but allow them to discover who they are – don't tell them who they are.

Here's how you do that. You allow them to start making decisions early on. You start with small decisions. When they're young, you start with "red cup or blue cup?" "Do you want to play inside or outside?" What you have is a person growing up making decisions based on what their internal desires are telling them rather than what we tell them.

Now, there comes a time where we have to provide direction and guidance on what might be a good choice. That is the balance of helping them discover who they are, not telling them who they are. That's one thing.

The second thing is we have to help them understand it's okay to make mistakes, but it's not okay to keep making them without seeking to change. Many times in our student culture, we allow students to make these mistakes and then make the statement — which I have come to hate – "That's just because they're teenagers" or "That's just because they're in college; that's what they do.

I've always thought that was a major copout, because, if we study student culture, many of the major inventions/movements throughout history were invented or started by teenagers and students. Whether you look at the invention of the snowmobile or the Glock 45 handgun, they were invented by teenagers and students in high school. We need to stop boxing them into a set of "This is what they do because …" and instead allow them to say, "There are no boundaries on how amazing I can be and what I accomplish…age is no limitation."

That leads me into my third thing, which is, I think we don't teach our students how to dream. And because of this, we don't teach them how to accomplish their dreams. For example, a young kid grows up and says, "I want to become a writer." A teacher might say, "Do you know how many people actually can make money as a writer? It's not that many." Automatically, a student thinks, "Well, I can't be a writer.

That's what I really want to do, but I can't do that because that's not realistic."

I remember I wanted to be a musician growing up, and I had a person who was a fairly successful musician say, "Less than one percent of people ever make it in music." I stopped playing my instrument.

We're training our students with that type of attitude to think immediately when they have a dream about why they can't accomplish it versus why they can. We're programming their subconscious mind whenever they have a dream or a vision to say, "It probably won't work because of this, this, this, and this," rather than asking the question, "How can I make it work? How can I do that?"

Imagine if all of our inventors throughout time, whether it is Thomas Edison or Henry Ford or any of these people that are attributed with great inventions, would have said, "Well, I probably can't invent the light bulb. I have failed hundreds, maybe thousands of times, so I have to stop." But they didn't.

What we have to do with our students is to start training them that when they come up with this crazy dream that's off the charts – "I want to run for President" — we start asking, "If you want to run for President, what kind of person do you think a President should be?" We start shaping them with questions. Start shaping their dreams and giving them ideas on how to accomplish it.

This is a fear of mine – I fear that we do that out of our own disgust with our own lack of success. Here's what I mean. I think oftentimes we're not happy with where we are or the choices we've made in our lives, so when a student or young adult comes up and says they want to accomplish a dream, our own cynicism and disgust with what we haven't accomplished we project on them instead of allowing them to really open the gates of their mind and run after anything they want.

Not only don't we allow students to dream, but also we don't teach them how to set and accomplish goals. To set the goal of, "I want to get these grades this year" or "I want to get into this school," and then help them develop plans on how to create it. We have students going on to college who have no idea how to set goals, which means they don't even have them. Without goals, you and I both know from studying success and experiencing some measure of success ourselves that success doesn't happen by accident.

I would say another thing a parent can do is help them. They're taking them to camp – ask them, "What do you want to get out of this camp? How do you want to grow because of it?"

If they're going to school – "What do you want to get out of this?" If they're playing a sport, an instrument, reading a book, writing a book, starting a club or organization on campus, at school, or in their community – "What do you want to get out of this? How do you want to see this change people?"

Asking questions like that turn our students into thinkers and doers, not just subjects of our environment.

There are small rewards and there are big rewards from my work. There are small rewards such as after I wrote my book, *Great Student Leaders Aren't Born, They're Made* and I spoke at some schools around the country and sold some copies, a small reward is one of the students in my audience posting on social media, "Just read Mike's book. It impacted me greatly." Those small rewards just seem that when I was buried in my office, stressed out about my writing project and I finally got it done ... those small rewards remind me that it was worth that; that I'm helping people. It's not just about creating a book to create revenue, which of course we hope for so that we can continue to further our mission, but it's one of those things where I'm making a difference. Those are some small things.

Bigger things are the results of going to Honduras just a few months ago and spending some time with children there that have been sponsored by some of our domestic sponsors that are sponsoring international students and children. I met a family. One of our sponsors had sponsored both of her children, and they were there and they had a little bag of corn, and that was all their food for the month. They ground up the corn, made tortillas, and that's all they ate for the month, because that's all they had.

Water was being delivered that day, and this is one of the things she said. "You know, it may not seem like much, but without our sponsors we wouldn't even have this." That kind of reward reminds me that our impact is not local. It's certainly global, but it's even greater than global – it's in the hearts of people, which change lives, which we have no idea what will change. It's literally that powerful. Those rewards are very, very rich.

19. Claiming Your Heroic Heart
Hal Price

Hal Price is the developer of Heroic Heart whose mission is to ignite the Divine Spark within the HEROIC HEART of children and their families by connecting them to their unique gifts and their authenticity while creating an inextricable bond between them.

The origins of Heroic Heart have been a lifetime in the making, but ultimately, it birthed itself on Monday, February 24, 2014 with a tremendous yank at Hal's heart at 4:25 am asking him how badly he wanted to stay on the planet to do what he came here to do!

As a recovering workaholic disguised as a highly successful Fortune 100 corporate branding and marketing executive, Hal hid his authentic self and his Divine gifts from the world for over 40 years. After spending 59 years of using his gifts and talents in service to others, Hal is now on time in rescuing his inner child to return joy, wisdom, and playfulness back into his world.

In 2013, surrounded by the death of both parents, malaise in his life, lack of fulfillment in his work, and a physical heart challenge, Hal set off on his transformational journey in February of 2014 to identify and claim his own heroic heart.
http://www.HeroicHeart.org

My Vision

My vision came from a place of seeing and experiencing a need in the world and then inviting grace and inner wisdom to inspire my heart to bring this idea forward.

Although I knew early on that my gifts of writing, telling stories and engaging hearts with wit and humor were a strength of mine, I had not made a concentrated effort to use my gifts for a higher purpose.

I had commoditized my writing to help companies, brands and celebrities tell their stories, but had never used my gifts to bring my heart forward to tell it's amazing story.

My inspiration came in the form of several simultaneous wake up calls that brought me to the stark realization that I had been living my life for everyone but me. In February of 2014, this pressure finally demanded that my heart be heard so, in a near "STROKE of genius," I was given a strong reminder that it was time for my gifts to be placed into service in a new and authentically "ME" way and to birth something bigger than me.

This reminder yanked me out of bed to take my blood pressure and I was shocked to see the numbers... 183/117... and climbing. My mind raced as fast as my heart with thousands of thoughts. Was I dying? Was I about to die alone with no one around me?

I immediately went to my closet to find my Living Trust and Will. I wrote a note on the document to my sister and placed the WILL at my door in case I did not make it through the night. As I walked away, I realized that I had long ago abandoned my WILL to be joyful and vibrant and I would need to pick up my own WILL to live. Then and there, I made a dramatic commitment to myself that I had never thought I needed to make...I WANTED TO LIVE and move back into my heart!

I chose to move from being a VICTIM to promising myself to become VITAL in every aspect of my life. I decided to release anything that was not serving my gift or my highest purpose. I had a long talk with my very caring boss and told him that I had to make changes in my life immediately. I told him that I loved him, but now I loved me more and needed to go in order to take care of myself.

After two months of medical tests and check-ups, I began a plan of recovery and self-nurturing to begin my journey to claim my HEROIC HEART. I asked spirit to come back and pour through me. I invited my parents and all my guardians and angels to help me create a vision.

I saw a world where children and their parents might come to know their gifts and their purpose on the planet. I wanted them to understand that there is a divine spark that's being called forward that wants to be revealed. That this could be developed, polished, nurtured and experienced. I wanted children to learn that they can connect with their gifts and true calling to create a world where they do what they love, they bring their joy and passion into the world, they support and encourage each other to follow that purpose all their lives, and that if they ever experience the pain of living disconnected from these gifts, that they have a way to get back.

HEROIC HEARTS grew from this place of WILLFUL LIVING, a PASSION for life and a JOYFUL COMMITMENT to let my gifts flow from me in each moment.

My Voyage

I have come to realize that there's an absolutely perfect gift that we're each given by our Creator that needs to be shared. So many of us are afraid to step into that gift, which is really our *superhero power*.

The more I thought about how I would bring that gift forward and remove all the "kryptonite" from my life, the more I realized that it was up to me to step out of fear and just know that I will be supported. There are miracles waiting to support me when I invite that gift to be placed into service.

The HEROIC HEART teaches that you are uniquely special among the seven billion people on the planet. We all have something significant to bring forward which becomes easier when we have the support of those who love us.

The HEROIC HEART is an opportunity for children and adults to remember who they are and then stand in their courage, overcome obstacles, and walk as an example for others.

Courage means 'strength of mind to carry on in spite of danger or difficulty'. It has its root from the French word curage, which means *heart*. That's what I'm inviting people to do with these books, this program, and the platform. To remember who they are and stand in their heart.

The Value of Lessons Learned

Having faced my challenge, I remembered that I am here to live in joy. I'm the "playground leader of the new world". That's my soul's branding statement – and this reclaimed position allows me to be more spontaneous.

I learned to ask for guidance and to get out of my own way and to remember that it's okay to make mistakes while I'm trying to move in a spiritual manner in the world.

I needed to remove fear and doubt. I learned that I am the only one ever stopping me from being grand.

This GRANDNESS is in all of us. We can each step into our glory at any moment. I now remember to pause before I make a decision and say, "In this breath, in this choice, in this word, in this action, is this serving my highest purpose?" When I move into that place of consciousness, I find that the things I am doing are much more delicious and mystical for me. Everything is aligned, and all of a sudden the higher purpose that I consciously chose to live allows my HEROIC HEART to expand and vibrate out to others.

The HEROIC HEART is currently being offered in two parts. One is a series of children's books that explore the journey of the heart. The other is our SuperHero Dream Camps for families who want to find a deeper connection with themselves and with one another.

The first book is about a bear cub named Eli whose mother gives birth to him prematurely at Bear Memorial Hospital. His heart is not fully developed. The doctors tell his mother that they need to take him to a human hospital called Heroic Hearts, which is 150 miles away. It's where kids go to have their hearts mended. Before he leaves, his mother sings him a lullaby, and that lullaby stays in his heart and mind the whole time he's away from her. Over time, he realizes that his desire to be with his mother and the people he loves is more important than getting his heart perfect. This love beckons him to begin the journey to travel homeward and reunite with his family.

While taking this journey (as in Joseph Campbell's "The Hero's Journey") his heart grows exponentially. With every step, as he moves into the unknown, he learns to trust his heart by listening to the song that serves as his inner guidance.

That's what I really want kids to know. That by becoming still and listening to their heart they gain access to the wisdom of the universe and are afforded higher insight into their inner truth and knowing.

In my story, Eli "Bear Behind" finally finds his mother by merely asking questions of his heart and listening to the song from his memory. In her joy to be reunited with her son, she promises to tell him a story every night about who he is, where he came from, and why he is so special.

She tells him about his heritage and the lineage that preceded him. He learns that each of his relatives helped change history by being authentic during brief encounters with historical people; and in this way, Eli also learns about key virtues of the heart.

Each book in the series reveals and models some of the key virtues of the heart such as forgiveness, compassion, patience, kindness, trust, acceptance, gratitude and vulnerability. As an emerging hero, Eli's heart continues to grow as he experiences the meaning and power of the lessons in each story.

With every story, kids get a merit sticker for their own HEROIC HEART badge that represent the virtues learned from the HEROIC HEART books. The goal of the series is to educate their young hearts to develop character, values and empathy. The books also serve as an introduction to the inspirational workshops at our SuperHero Dream Camp where they will learn:

1. Who they are
2. Why they're special
3. What gift they have to offer the world
4. How to follow their passion and create their dreams
5. How to be supported by one another as a family unit to create a memorable, inextricable bond.

Words of Wisdom and Vision

Many of us disconnect way too early from the inner child who is precious beyond measure. Each child's birthright is to find joy in living, wonder in each moment and access their creative imagination. As a competitive species, we are driven by ambition and the ego's need to out-do others. Ultimately, we forget that this divine spark just wants to come play, learn, grow, love, and make a difference in the world.

We benefit from understanding that there is a unique gift and calling that everybody has, and nobody can do it the way you're going to do it. It's not to be better than others, but it's *your personal best*. My goal is to help others develop their connection to their calling so they can acknowledge it and live it. This gives meaning to their lives and a sense of true value.

I am blessed by the numerous teachers who have influenced my spiritual awakening. Each one arrived at the precise moment I was ready to take new steps on my journey.

From these teachings, a number of practices developed, which allow me access to connect to the wisdom of my inner child. I walk in nature. I do a number of heart alignment and trusted source meditations. I listen to joyful, uplifting music and I journal. I like to hang out with kids and adults who remind me of the power of an open heart.

Mystical insights now come to me from my everyday surroundings. For some, this may sound strange – but I started seeing license plates displaying the initials of a dear deceased friend. Those initials, AKP, got my attention. I soon realized that the numbers that followed the initials were messages being given to me from a higher source.

There is also magic in the people that come into your life. They're there for a reason. They're there to teach you, guide you, mirror your thoughts, support you and challenge your beliefs. Really study yourself. The old saying, "To thine own self be true" or "Know thyself," I think is so important. The power of my near-death experience flooded over me like crazy. I cried for a day just feeling how precious I really was and had an awareness for the first time of the gift I had to bring into the world.

I began to study who I AM, why I'm unique, and what gifts I had been given. Once I saw all of me, I was able to craft a blueprint of my own divine essence and see my mission here very clearly.

I love writing. I love telling stories. I love making children laugh because they make me laugh. I encourage you to find out what brings you joy. Discover what brings that sense of levity and brightness to you and watch the miracles show up.

Just know that there's nothing that blocks you except for you. Please look for your sources of inspiration and find yourself again. Start writing and recording your thoughts, what makes you feel good and what you love doing. Then DO THAT! That's what is working for me. Honestly, every time I take this little bear called Eli "Bear Behind" out into the world, he is my inner child inviting miracles to appear in my life to show me how glad he is that I reclaimed MYSELF and my JOY.

Blessings to you all in finding your gift and claiming your HEROIC HEART!

20. ACT ON LOVE™
Dr. Mamiko Odegard

Dr. Mamiko Odegard has helped thousands of individuals and couples become happy, loving, and enjoying success with her over 30 years experience as a coach, psychologist, and therapist.

You will be inspired by Mamiko's "practice what you preach" approach to loving and accepting yourself and others. As the best-selling author of *Daily Affirmations for Love: 365 Days of Love in Thought and Action,* she is happily married to Greg, the love of her life for over 40 years. She is also Strathmore's Who's Who Worldwide Life Coach for 2012. Greg and Mamiko were also honored as the Couple of the Week on the Dr. Laura Berman Show, Oprah Radio.

Offering life-changing insights and results for immediate change, Mamiko's trademark has become her ability to quickly gain amazing results in days and weeks—not months or years! Find out for yourself, by contacting her at 480-391-1184 or emailing her at DrMamiko@ACTonlove.com.

My Vision

My passion is to enable each of you to recognize and believe that you are EXTRAordinary and that you deserve to have the ultimate love relationship. I want you to experience the joy, love, freedom, peace, opportunities, and successes that open for you when you fully accept and love yourself.

Only when you have a love affair with yourself, can you attract and keep a relationship in which you are cherished and treated as the most important person in another's life. Speaking from my own experience with a marriage of over 40 years, I can assure you that you don't have to forsake a prosperous, invigorating career to have a loving and passionate relationship where your partner encourages and supports your business success and celebrates life with you.

Unfortunately, as many of us have become successful in pursuing our professional passions, more of us are experiencing increased strains in our relationships. As a powerful woman, you're noticing that it's more difficult for you to attract a man, and especially difficult to find and keep a committed relationship. In recent years as we women have become more successful and empowered at work, relationships with our love partners have become more jeopardized. About 50% of all marriages end in divorce, and more women are engaging in affairs as opportunities increase for travel and interactions with business associates. Do you know how to keep your romantic relationship alive while pursuing your path to career success?

Some of you give up on your dreams of combining a family and career; some merely focus more and dedicate more energy to your profession while hoping deep inside that a miracle happens in which your leading man magically appears. Others might "settle," marrying someone so you have a companion in your life, or fill the desperate need to marry just to have the child that you want so badly.

But you don't have to settle! I want to give you hope and a blueprint so you can have it all: Love and career success. My life and our marriage are a testament that you can have all your heart and mind desire, and I want you to know and feel the joy, love, and fulfillment that is waiting for you.

My Voyage

I met my husband, Greg, the love of my life, at Colorado State University. I was in my last year of undergraduate school and he was just beginning his doctoral studies. At the beginning of our relationship and in the early days of our marriage, I thought of Greg as being the older and wiser one who seemed to possess so much knowledge of our environment, history, and current social events. He was a great teacher to me about the natural sciences and continually helped me to expand my vocabulary and knowledge while providing ongoing encouragement for all that I pursued.

While Greg and I dated, he was convinced that I would truly be happy if he would take care of me as a "housewife." His mother had long instilled in him that the road to happiness was for a woman to be taken care of financially so she could be the homemaker. Despite our discussions to the contrary that I wanted to work and my belief and commitment that I could contribute to the well-being of others, Greg held onto his old beliefs. This changed almost immediately after we married and I brought home my first paycheck. All the sudden, he thought being a dual career couple was the best of all worlds, allowing us to have the financial benefit of two incomes and easing the burden on him as the "breadwinner."

Early on in our relationship, we encountered a major potential conflict. One of our first arguments was about division of labor. Since both of us were working and going to school, I wanted more of Greg's help with home responsibilities. Greg, on the other hand, thought I should be assuming more of the domestic chores. It was right then and there that we decided that we needed to better define and divide up our roles to maintain an equal balance in which we both helped with chores so that we could efficiently and democratically have time for study and leisure activities.

Two years after our marriage, we both graduated on the same day; Greg with his Ph.D. and I with my Masters. We were thrilled to be starting our professional careers with Greg getting a fabulous offer from an energy company. We moved back east and I started my job as a counselor at a private junior college. We felt on top of the world, being gainfully employed, but Greg was the greater financial contributor even after I had taken on a position as Director of Counseling at a private university.

Greg had a huge career boost a few years later when he directed another energy company, allowing me to fully concentrate on pursuing my Ph.D. Life was now even more exciting and fun for us with Greg's position and my teaching college after I attained my doctorate.

However, a major shift happened when we decided to further our career opportunities and to have greater freedom in where we lived. Greg quit his lucrative job and enrolled as a full-time law student. I opened up a psychology practice in Scottsdale, Arizona. For the first time, I became the sole "breadwinner." The financial pressures to succeed were immense. Even as our roles became dramatically different, we still were fairly egalitarian. I laugh when I say this, because I once called Greg on a Sunday morning while he was studying and I was house hunting. I found what I thought was our "dream home" and called him saying that he might want to come and look at a particular home because I was about to make an offer on it. He quickly responded that he didn't want me to do anything until he got there. Although this is an extreme example, I felt so comfortable and confident in our relationship that Greg would give his blessing to my decisions. This example was indicative of how we could be our own persons, while still communicating about decisions and supporting one other. Then and now, this is our modus operandi for mutually helping each other advance our careers as well as loving, understanding, and encouraging the other to "go for it!" And yes, we did purchase the beautiful home. Even to this day, we respect and ask for each other's opinions on such things as business strategies, presentations, and editing the others' professional documents.

Happily, Greg's gutsy decision to return to school paid off, and he became an officer in his previous company. However, I had my practice in Arizona and his employer was in Texas. Greg commuted home every weekend for 27 years as we loved living in Scottsdale and I loved being an entrepreneur, helping others!

As both of our careers developed and flourished, various struggles emerged with keeping the communication, intimacy, and passion vibrant, while employing different parenting styles with our daughter. After almost 20 years of marriage as "dinks," (dual income no kids), our daughter, Mariesa, was born. I then began a life as a "single parent" during the week because of Greg's commuting out of state for his job. In contrast, our weekends together were often like honeymoon celebrations that also included Greg's one-on-one time with our daughter, our family time, and personal time for myself. It became imperative to cooperate together even more and if there were disagreements, our time together during weekends was too precious to have it ruined by tension, frustration, and anger.

We were in bliss for many years on all fronts until we faced an additional challenge: unemployment. Greg was let go due to downsizing. Because of his executive position and scarcity of jobs in his field, he went through the strains of unemployment three times, sometimes for prolonged periods. Each time, I again had to assume the role of the primary breadwinner resulting in stress for us both. The crucial role of honest communication, the many daily demonstrations of love, appreciation, emotional support, and physical contributions for each other as life partners, best friend, lover, and parent has kept our relationship vibrant and loving. A healthy dose of laughter and having fun in our lives is also essential in loving each other, feeling gratitude for our life, and perpetuating our "being in love with love" through our many years together while overcoming our life struggles.

The Value of Lessons Learned

As a love and relationship expert, I now realize that I have spent my entire life building self-esteem and developing deep personal relationships. I learned to be warm, easily approachable, affectionate, a great listener and friend, expressive, and demonstrated acts of caring and thoughtfulness towards those around me. My first step and the only control I truly had were to create the best version of myself. In reality, Greg was attracted to me and found me irresistible because I took personal responsibility to feel secure and was affirming of myself.

I also recognized the importance of nurturing YOU³: The three key relationships we each have –

- The relationship with ourselves;
- The relationship with others - family, friends, co-workers, and acquaintances; and
- The relationship with our romantic love partner.

To be truly successful in life, love, and business, we must learn how to fully develop each type of relationship.

As women, we have greatly emerged in numbers and escalating levels of power and influence with over 57% of women working, according to the 2013 Bureau of Labor Statistics. Among the numbers, we have taken great strides in leadership in corporate settings as well as in the entrepreneurial arena.

Unfortunately, side effects for career success among women can be experienced as:

1. Remaining single longer;
2. Having more difficulty attracting and keeping relationships;
3. Experiencing more conflicts and strains at home;
4. Losing a sense of femininity;
5. Greater involvement in affairs; and
6. Increasing chances of separation or divorce.

Let's take a look at your typical day to see how pervasively you may be unconsciously losing your femininity. When you wake up in the morning, you are already making checklists on your "to do list." Even as you drive to work, you are in your masculine energy, analyzing the best routes, watching traffic signals, streaming on the road with other cars, and monitoring how fast you drive. At work, you are primarily in your male role, making decisions, preparing for meetings, and directing others what to do.

As women, we are making more choices at work and at home...and each time we feel more emboldened, stimulating us to be even more empowered. Your man may intellectually support your newfound power and status, but you might notice that he is more quiet, aloof, or doing his own activities. He may no longer feel like a central figure in your life. Perhaps you have noticed that he's not as affectionate...and perhaps that has happened to you...the lack of conscious loving insidiously creeping into your life as you feel more of your attention diverted to work and blurring the roles of wife or girlfriend versus professional.

Words of Wisdom and Vision

What's the solution? The solution is to create your best self and to use conscious loving by being aware and dancing to both your male and female energies. Just like ballroom dancing, the pacing and changes in who leads and follows, is choreographed and coordinated to flow together. Your man wants to be the source of strength for you; he wants to make decisions or at least be included in the decisions you make.

Here's a quick ACT-ivity that you can do. Take a sheet of paper and list various characteristics that describe YOU. Then go through your list and decide whether each is primarily a male characteristic or female. Look through your checkmarks to determine whether you are more traditionally male or female.

You might be surprised to note that you are an exquisite blend of male and female characteristics. This represents personal androgyny; and the healthiest person, psychologically, possesses both male and female traits. Ah, the perfect ying and yang to go with the flow.

The secret to really boosting your loving connection with a partner, even if you are out of balance is to **"consciously love."** What does this mean? First you are taking responsibility for becoming the best you and taking steps to create more love in your life. You can start now to "ACT on Love™" several times daily.

The following seven ways help you show love to yourself and others in various ways throughout the day:

- Demonstrate **physical affection** by hugging, kissing, holding hands, snuggling, stroking or brushing the other's hair, or massaging the neck, shoulders, and feet. This is not about sex, but being more attuned to our need to be physically connected and valued.
- Show **verbal affection** through complimenting, appreciating, recognizing, and saying words of love, "I love you," "You're perfect for me," "I can't believe I'm married to you," "I'm the luckiest woman alive to have you in my life," or "You look so sexy and handsome," are ways to turn up love and happiness for your loved one.

- **Acts of love or labor of love** are those thoughtful considerate behaviors that make another's life easier. It could be making coffee and bringing it to your partner, taking out the garbage without being asked, filling up gas for the car, or washing the car to keep it looking like new. "**Love is a verb**" is an easy way of remembering acts of kindness.
- **Quality of time** means making your time together meaningful and special whether it is laughing together, watching and rooting for your favorite team, or engaging in an activity together that is mutually enjoyable and fun that stimulates your mind or body. It can also be quiet time to snuggle as you hold each other close or to discuss meaningful topics.
- **Giving gifts** have long been a way of showing affection. Whether they are poems, love notes, jewelry, clothing, or a favorite sweet delicacy, either bought or made...they include anything that surprises, pleases and creates appreciation for your beloved.
- One of the best ways to demonstrate love is to truly **hear and understand** each other. When you "get him" and vice versa, it is a time of supreme connectedness. When you mirror the other's feelings and describe in your own words what the experience must be like for your partner, then it leads to the deepest form of love, that of "intimacy."
- **Intimacy** is the ability to give and receive love and to be so comfortable with your partner that you can be your true self. Each of you are authentic and transparent about your thoughts, feelings, needs, and wants such as what you wish for your relationship, what creates

sadness, frustration, disappointment, insecurity, and worries as well as happiness, excitement, hope, and love. Intimacy is the deepest way we can show how much we love another, by being vulnerable with our feelings and what we want and need in order for our lover to fully understand, to have empathy, and to respond to us in kind.

If you are ever blessed to be able to experience deep understanding and intimacy as both the giver and receiver, you have found your soul mate. This substantially increases your chances for keeping your love as you succeed in business, and certainly in your life. Love is not a matter of chance; it is all about conscious loving of yourself and others.

Start now to have fun and to ACT on Love™ to see your love, your life, and your business blossom.

Voyage to Wellness

21. Heal Through Humor
Allen Klein

Allen Klein is an award-winning professional speaker who offers humor and tips about dealing with change, challenge, and stress in the workplace. Allen is the author of *The Healing Power of Humor*, currently in its 40th printing and ninth language translation. Allen has authored 20 best-selling books about humor as well as motivational and inspirational books about the positive side of life.

Allen has received the Lifetime Achievement Award from the Association of Applied and Therapeutic Humor, a Toastmasters Communication and Leadership Award, a Certified Speaking Professional Designation from the National Speakers Association, and is a Hunter College Hall of Fame honoree.

The way to spell relief is L-A-U-G-H. No wonder people call Allen the "Jollytologist®!" humor@allenklein.com

My Vision

The title "Jollytologist" came because I actually have a Master's degree in Human Development, and my thesis was "The Healing Power of Humor," which turned into my first book, although the writing is very different than my thesis.

I got into therapeutic humor by what some people would say was a tragic situation. My wife passed away at 34. She had a terminal illness, a rare liver disease. At 31, we found out about that. She had a great sense of humor. During those difficult three years, she would use humor. There were lots of tears, but there was also laughter.

I'll give you one example. She was in the hospital with a copy of *Playgirl* magazine with the male nude centerfold, and she said, "Allen, I really like this picture this month. Can you put it on the wall by the bed over there?" I said, "Ellen, this is a hospital. It's a little risqué for that."

She said, "Why don't you get a leaf from the plant over there and cover up that part?" I did that and things were fine for the first day, fine for the second day, but by the third day the leaf started shriveling up! It was a difficult time, but we would look at that picture or we would think of that picture and we would start to laugh.

After Ellen passed away, I realized it wasn't a lot of laughter, but there was five or ten seconds, and it helped us rise above the situation, gave us a reprieve, and gave us a perspective that humor always gives you when you can find some humor in a situation.

I thought, "What a powerful tool that was to help cope with difficult situations." Yet, hardly anyone ever talked about humor in death and dying situations.

I went back to school. I got the Master's degree in Human Development, and that turned into my first book, *The Healing Power of Humor*. It also led to a whole new career of being a keynote speaker and workshop leader talking about the therapeutic value of humor.

My Voyage

In my workshops, I ask people how many people can remember a joke or a good joke teller? I would say maybe five people out of 100 might raise their hands; but one thing we can always do is just look around and have a reminder, something to remind us to lighten up when things aren't going well.

I'm real partial to a prop, a reminder, a sign, a photograph. For instance, everyone in my programs gets a sponge red rubber clown nose, because when they're not doing too well on a day, if they put that on and look in the mirror, it's hard to not laugh. Or, if they're having an argument with someone, if they put it on, chances are the argument will stop.

It's just this little prop to remember to lighten up; or you can have a feather on the dashboard of your car to remind you to lighten up when you're in traffic jams; or, have a funny photo around. I have a photo of my daughter when she was a teenager and wanted a pie thrown in her face. She is just glowing with joy when that happened. A sign can help you lighten up too. I have a sign in my office that says, "Never wrestle with a pig – you both get dirty and the pig likes it."

I make a differentiation between humor and laughter. I go to humor conferences where there are people who do scientific research. They get really deep into what humor/laughter means, but I like to keep things simple. For me, humor is seeing something in a humorous way, which in turn gets you to laugh. Laughter then is the physical expression of finding something funny.

For me, it's almost like changing your attitude, looking at something differently, trying to find the lighter side of something difficult or something that irritates you. Then, the laughter is the physical expression of that humor.

I put together a program that's called "Seeing Demise Through Humorous Eyes." It's how cartoonists, comedians, and cinematographers show us how we can lighten up about death, how we can see death as less of a grave matter.

What they do is they take death and dying situations, and they see the absurdity in some of it. We all know that yes, it's a serious situation, but humor helps us cope. We have all gone to funerals where we're crying one minute and maybe laughing at someone's comment the next. Maybe they look in the coffin and say, "Oh, he's never looked so good," which is kind of absurd.

Yes, death and dying is serious, but I'm not sure it has to be solemn. I think if we can find the humor even there, it's helping us cope. One quick research that I found —-Dacher Keltner wrote a book about his research with spouses that had lost their significant other, their spouse. If they found some humor within the first couple of months after their loved one died, they did much better over a two-year period than people who did not find anything to lighten up about after the death of their spouse.

We don't think about humor or laughter and losing someone, but yet it seems to be very beneficial. I think what it shows survivors is they can cope. It's a difficult situation, but they can go on with their life and they can enjoy life again after the loss.

The Value of Lessons Learned

It's funny – whether I'm doing a 20-minute presentation (which I've done, flown all the way across the country to do 20 minutes) or whether I'm doing a one-hour or six-hour workshop, I build it all on the letters **L-A-U-G-H** so that people can remember when they leave the workshop some of the tools they can use to find the humor in their work and their life.

L is **let go**. It's a very Zen kind of thing to let go. If you're holding on to anything – anger, frustration, upset, you can't laugh about it. So the very first notion to get more laughter in your life is to let go. I lead the audience in a lot of playful exercises in the workshop. One of them is, if you're angry with your boss or your kid or your spouse, get a balloon and blow that anger into the balloon and release it. It's a simple way of starting to let go of that anger. You've got to let go to find the laughter. It's amazing when you see an audience of 500 balloons going around the room. It's so fabulous and memorable.

A – (I just touched on that a little while ago) – is **attitude**. Basically, finding humor is switching your attitude. Viktor Frankl talks about that, finding humor in a concentration camp, and it helped him survive.

U – (I cheated a little here) –-is "**y-o-u**" – you need to change your attitude; you need to let go. No one else can do it for you.

G – is **go do it**. In *The Healing Power of Humor* book, I have 14 techniques. I go through some of activities with the audience.

H – it's really simple – open your humor eyes and ears and look for **humor**, because it is all around.

For example, I was in a Laundromat last week and I looked on the wall and there was a sign. It said, "When the machine stops, remove all your clothing." There is humor all around, but we get so stressed out we don't see it. That's what I talk about.

As I mentioned, after my wife's passing, I realized she had such a great sense of humor, and how that humor helped me cope. There was laughter and tears, but it was the laughter that momentarily helped me get a little perspective and get on with the situation. I wanted to share that with the world. I had this passion to share the incredible power of therapeutic humor.

By the way, I almost failed speech in college. I think I got a D or a D-. I did not like getting up in front of a group to speak, but I had this passion to tell people, "Hey folks, you need to lighten up. No matter what the situation, look for the humor." I had to share this with the world both in speaking and then certainly in writing to get the book to a bigger audience.

I realized that one book – and this is for the authors in the audience who are reading this – that one book can get you more coverage, you can get your message to more people than you can with probably all the speeches in your life, even if you're the most popular speaker in the world, because that book gets passed on, gets read over and over and over.

It was really a passion that I had to get this book out. It wasn't easy. It took several years. And midway, there was a change of editor. But I had this passion to tell the world about the therapeutic value of humor so I just kept plugging away. And I'm so glad I did, because now I get letters of how it helped people and how it's changed their life.

I also put together seven or eight books containing almost 500 inspirational/motivational quotations each. I think what's so great about quotations is that it puts a great deal of knowledge in just this little nut that you can digest pretty quickly. The latest book is *Having the Time of Your Life: Little Lessons To Live By*.

I think words are so powerful, particularly in affirmations or quotations, because you can't remember a whole book, but you can remember a little part of a quotation, and it could help you with your life or how to get on with your day.

Words of Wisdom and Vision

My wife had a great comment that I still remember. She said, "Sometimes in life what we don't get in our childhood, we get in our later years." I was a very serious child. The older I become, the more playful, the more joy I seem to attract. I've become more childlike.

My wife's passing started me on my path as a writer; I had to share my message about therapeutic humor. My personal story is, "Look, I am grieving. I have a 10-year-old daughter. Her mother, my wife is dying, and yet there is humor here, and that humor is helping us get through the difficult situations."

22. Crisis Response
Denise Joy Thompson

Founder and owner of Crisis Response Consulting, **Denise Joy Thompson** is a licensed clinical social worker and a graduate of Florida State University. As a lieutenant colonel in the U.S. Air Force Reserve, she served over eleven years of active duty, including two deployments, following September 11, 2001.

During this period of active duty, Denise served as Chief Sexual Assault Prevention and Response Deployment Operations, and five years as Chief Behavioral Health for the U.S. Air Force Reserve Command Surgeon General.

Crisis Response Consulting is an organization dedicated to strengthening crisis and disaster response resources, building resiliency and enhancing support to first responders, individuals affected by traumatic events, communities, and organizations through consultations, education, and training. www.crisisresponseconsulting.com

My Vision

There's a lot going on in our world today that is very traumatic and disturbing, and affects a large number of individuals. Working with people affected by trauma has become my talent and gift, which I am able to share with those in need of support and a listening ear.

It is difficult in a few sentences to describe 25 years of working with individuals who needed support after a traumatic event. When I first became a social worker, I didn't know I was going to spend most of my career in trauma.

I have provided support to children and adults who have been physically and sexually abused. I've spent 23 years providing support in the military, dealing not only with combat-related PTSD, but sexual assault-related PTSD and other mental health issues. Over the last 12 years, I've concentrated on providing support to first responders – police officers, EMS, firefighters, disaster workers, who have experienced traumatic events.

My Voyage

It's interesting how I became involved in social work. I grew up in a small town in Iowa and was very involved in our Lutheran Church. I taught Sunday school and Bible school, was involved in the choir and youth group. In my senior year, we had a female pastor, who was a very good role model and mentor. At that time, I didn't know what I wanted to do in my life. I thought about doing something within the church and decided to attend a Lutheran college for my undergraduate degree, and I did think about going into the seminary.

As I thought about what I should do, how best to help people, looking at all my options and talking to different professors, it seemed going into ministry and attending seminary was not the answer. The right decision at the time was social work. If I felt ministry was the right path, then I could choose to follow that path in the future. With a plan in mind of how to assist large numbers of people, I completed my undergraduate degree in social work.

I love education and learning, so following my graduation I thought, "I need to add more to my skills than what I have." I decided to go to Florida State University for my Master's degree in Social Work. It was ironic, because I told my parents and my professors, "I applied for Florida State, and that's where I'm going to go."

They said, "Did you only apply to one graduate program?"

I said, "Yes, but they have a really good program, and that's where I want to go. I only applied there. Why? Is that a problem?"

They said, "Normally, people don't get accepted to their first choice. That's why they apply to several different universities." I said, "But I don't want to go anywhere else. That's where I'm going to go." This has been a pattern in my life to set my sights on what I want and to do it!!!!

Luckily, I was accepted. I went into a clinical program and spent my "free-time" working with homeless individuals and individuals with lower socioeconomic status. My clinical internship was in a VA hospital working with veterans, mainly from the Vietnam era. Early on in my career I worked with trauma-related issues, PTSD and other chronic mental health illnesses.

I thought, "This is where I'm supposed to be. This is supposed to be my focus, working with individuals who have trauma-related mental health and life issues." That started my career in trauma. I've been a therapist now for 25 years. I followed a path in how I could use my services and then it was decided that was not where I needed to go. No one necessarily decided that for me; it was just a sense and a feeling I had to go down a different path. My career is a ministry, just not within a church.

It comes back to having a sense of fulfillment. I am able to use my education and my interpersonal skills to talk someone through a difficult time in their life. If a person doesn't receive support to work through it, we know the event can become so overwhelming a person may become dysfunctional. Or worse, with depression, PTSD or a significant level of anxiety, a person may become suicidal.

To me, it's giving of my time, but it's also being a lifesaver for someone else. This has been a motivating factor in continuing for over 25 years working in the field of trauma, making sure people are linked to resources, and there's an avenue to talk with somebody to process what has happened.

Most of the time when asked, military members and first responders want to continue doing their job. No matter what they have experienced, no matter what has affected them, no matter what they have faced in their job, they are still committed to doing their job, because their job is saving other people's lives.

One of the things in dealing with military members especially and talking to people who have had multiple deployments is oftentimes they say, "But I'm ready to go back." No matter what they're struggling with today, no matter what their injuries may be, there's still this sense of commitment, and there's this sense of mission, they still want to go back and finish the job they think is not finished yet. They want to go back and do the best they can, because they realize what they do saves lives and helps others.

When I talk to those individuals and their motivation is to keep on going it's like, "This is how I can support them." I can keep going also. What I do behind the scenes, one-on-one or with groups of individuals who have been affected, is support them in continuing their mission. That's one of the significant motivating factors for me to continue to do what I'm doing.

The Value of Lessons Learned

People ask me, "What do you do for a living?" I say, "I work and provide crisis and disaster response." They'll say, "What do you do for hobbies?" I jokingly say, "I provide crisis and disaster response."

I also volunteer on a team where we support nonprofit organizations and volunteer first responder departments who don't have support through an insurance company. In some ways, and in and talking to other people who do similar work, it can be difficult at times to remove yourself from that world, to remove yourself from that's all you're doing, seeing, thinking, and being.

I think one of the challenges is to specifically have other hobbies, other interests, and other friends outside of that world. If you don't, you're always talking about the same thing. We'll joke when you have a bunch of first responders or crisis responders together and you see people getting up from the table next to you, you know you probably were a little bit too graphic about the last response you had. We're used to talking about disaster, death and things like that over lunch, dinner or at happy hour, but other people aren't necessarily used to that.

Sometimes I have to be careful of, "Is this my whole world?" The challenge is to do something else outside of "trauma".

One of the things I try to do is meditate on a daily basis. I try to take a "time out", and have time to center myself, quiet my mind, get into a very peaceful, relaxed state before I start the day, because I never quite know what the day is going to look like.

Also, as much as possible, and I recommend to everybody else because it's a healthy thing to do, is incorporate exercise into my week. Usually, I don't exercise every day; but four to five times a week, I make sure I'm exercising.

I also try and limit the amount of TV. I've done a better job the last several years in not watching too much news. Our news today, even though I want to give journalists credit in sometimes trying to focus on the positive, seems to always have such a negative perspective or is traumatic, because there are so many things going on in our world today. The more we view and focus on in the news or in reading which has a negative perspective, then the more negativity permeates our thoughts. It permeates our thoughts and can affect our mood. Because I know I'm going to deal with that in my professional life, I try to limit the exposure to negativity and trauma when I have downtime.

Also, I talk to my friends. Again, a lot of my friends are in the first responder world, so on one hand that's very helpful, because they have an understanding if I need to process a particularly difficult response or call or dealing with a client or patient. I can process that with them, so we have that common understanding.

My family is a very good support system. I know whenever I need to talk to any of my family members, I can reach out to them and they're going to be supportive and listen to what I have to say; not necessarily give me advice or tell me what to do, but be a sounding board.

I love to take vacations!! I don't have as many as I would like, but spending time on the beach is one of my favorite things to do. It really allows me to relax and take some time out and get rejuvenated and ready for whatever I might face the next day.

Words of Wisdom and Vision

One of the things people can do is accept the trauma or what has happened does not define them. Yes, a traumatic incident has happened. It can be a traumatic loss of life, it could be sexual assault, it could be combat-related – whatever the trauma or significant situation is. Even though at the time it is so devastating and overwhelming for them, if they take a step back and realize there are going to be thoughts and memories, but it doesn't have to impact and negate who the person was before the incident. What were their skills? What were their talents? What were their gifts? What were their dreams? This event does not have to take all of that away.

It might take them time, a few months or longer, to put this incident into perspective, and it will probably take talking to somebody, whether it's a pastor, therapist, or a coach, but they can put it into a perspective which allows them to live their life and to live a fulfilling life.

Oftentimes when people are hit with a significant tragedy, they don't see a future for themselves. The reality is, we always have a future. It may be different than what we had envisioned, it may be different than what we had wanted, but we are always capable of creating a new future. Sometimes, when we're in the midst of tragedy, the pain and our sense of loss, we lose sight of what we have accomplished in the past, and we have the ability to accomplish a future.

My biggest recommendation would be for people, who are experiencing something significant and devastating in their lives, remember there are people out there prepared and available to help them through the situation, even though there's pain in processing and moving forward.

There are many resources for individuals who are dealing with significant loss, whether it's a loss to themselves or loss of someone close to them. I think the best thing a person can do is to reach out to others. This is really the most important action to take, instead of stagnating, staying stuck. It's almost like walking ourselves into our house and we don't ever go out again – we know that is not helpful or healthy. Even though the suggestions are simple, opening up and talking can be one of the most difficult steps to take. Talking and reaching out are the main things to do when somebody is dealing with trauma or significant loss.

23. Realize Your True Value
Dr. Francesca A. Jackson

Dr. Francesca A. Jackson founded a clinical practice in Bay Area, California, and specialized in seeing people who had been given up on, and told they would have to 'learn to live with it.'

She has maintained a daily personal practice of meditation and techniques using yoga and science of the breath for over 38 years, and has been teaching these techniques for the past 19 years.

She has worked with people facing their mortality – including cancer and HIV – also with incarcerated individuals (men, women, juveniles in all security levels) and people struggling to recover from trauma (veterans, earthquake in Haiti, Hurricane Katrina). mynewlife108@gmail.com

My Vision

Right now I'm in the middle of a major life transition. In March, I decided to change the life that I was living. I stopped doing what I was doing. I'd been working for a humanitarian nonprofit basically on a stipend for a number of years and decided I needed to do things in a different way, so I changed the course of my life.

I want to keep contributing. I'm looking at ways to take all the skills that I have and put them together into a new package that I can offer. One of the bylines that I have for myself is "I will walk in the dark and turn on the light." I think that, not only in this country but the world at large, there is a lot of untapped potential that we throw away. I don't think we can afford that, given the way that the world is. There are a lot of people who have been marginalized; a lot of people who have believed that what they have to offer is not of value unless it comes in a certain package, unless it looks a certain way.

What I do is teach people different techniques that are self-administered and self-empowering, bring people back into their own strength, bring people to being able to honor what they know and honor who they are, and take their gifts and create them into a package that they can then give to the world.

My Voyage

By profession, I'm a chiropractor and a homeopath. I had a private practice in the Bay area for a number of years. I was beginning my practice as the AIDS epidemic came. At the same time the AIDS epidemic was happening, the women's breast cancer epidemic was also happening. I worked with those two populations quite a bit in my private practice.

For myself, I've been meditating regularly for nearly 40 years. After being in private practice for about 14 years, I decided that I wanted to do my work in the nonprofit sector. The beauty of it was that it allowed me to travel and be able to work with people on the margins.

I taught in correctional facilities from probation school to maximum security, all the way to men who had been in solitary confinement and were earning their way back to maximum security. I was teaching in the HIV community, working with veterans with PTSD, and female veterans with military sexual trauma. I had the opportunity to teach in Haiti before and after the earthquake, in Senegal, in Botswana, and in South Africa. I'm not sure that I would have had the opportunity to do that in the same way had I just been in my private practice. That was very fortunate for me. I was happy to be able to do that, and learned a lot from being able to do that.

The Value of Lessons Learned

When you've gotten through something that's excruciatingly challenging, what you learn becomes your wealth. Once it becomes your wealth, then it is knowledge that you have to teach to someone else.

I was homeless when I went through chiropractic school. I lived in my car for a year-and-a-half. I come from very humble beginnings. I came from a military family. I didn't really grow up with anything that in this day and age we would call privileged and advantaged. What I learned from those life circumstances is to find the strength and resilience inside you to keep going.

Meditation and breathing techniques helped me enormously. People give up – people who haven't had someone to help them, people who have gone through hard circumstances. It's very easy to lose your way, to give up, because we haven't been taught basic skills on handling mind and emotions. We live in an intense world that is moving faster than we can keep up with.

I think that a lot of the world suffers from posttraumatic stress. A lot of people are living in very difficult circumstances. When I worked with gang kids, it was at a time when gang culture was really raging. They told me just walking back and forth to school was dangerous. For many people who are living in inner cities or in war zones, everyday life is a challenge. If there are whole generations with that experience, then how do you get the inner strength to keep going? If everyone who looks at you, everyone that you encounter in some way has made a decision as to whether or not you have value, and they impart that decision to you, you ingest that decision and decide, "Maybe I don't have value," it's very hard to keep going.

Wealth comes in all different forms. There are a lot of people who have a lot of money but feel like they have no meaning in their life. I have no understanding of that because there's so much need in this world. There are so many ways that you can contribute to other people. All you have to do is just pick something, do it, keep going and don't stop.

I don't really think so much about leaving a legacy myself. In 100 years, practically every person who is alive on this planet will be forgotten. Nobody's going to even remember that they were ever here. Everything that you do has an impact and a ripple throughout the world. That is what remains, whether anyone remembers you or not.

When I first started looking at Eastern principles 40 years ago - meditation, yoga, breathing techniques - it was not a popular thing. People looked at you as though you had lost your mind and you were on the fringe. Now, of course, practically everybody knows what those things are, whether or not it is a path they choose.

I see a lot of narcissism in the world right now; at the same time, I see that people are beginning to look and see that we must make some major, major changes, and that those changes are not all necessarily external. For everything that we do or want to do, there is an internal solution. Making yourself strong and resilient from the inside, and seeking guidance from there, gives you an ability to not only make changes in your own life, but in the lives of the people around you.

I think that people need to put their cell phones down more. I sit on street corners a lot and watch people crossing the street in the intersection, and everybody is looking down; everyone is looking at their cell phone. When I teach workshops, I always ask people, "How many people here want world peace?" and, of course, everybody raises their hand. I say, "Do you think there's an app for that? Because if you don't put your cell phone down, if you can't talk to the person who is sitting right next to you, if you can't be friendly to the people who are living in your same neighborhood, then how is world peace ever going to happen? There's not an app that you can download for that. *You are the app.*"

We have an Internet that allows us to talk with people in

nanoseconds around the world. We need to begin to be able to do that with the people who are standing right next to us, and see that all of us are really part and parcel of each other. If we really, truly believe that, then we need to act like it.

Words of Wisdom and Vision

Before I give anybody any advice on anything, I listen to what it is they have to say. Everyone is in a different place. My perspective is that not one solution fits all. Everyone is in a different place, and everyone has different needs. You can say something to one person and they'll run; another person can only take a baby step. That baby step may be the same step that they're taking for months or years.

There are many, very easy breathing techniques that I teach people. Without our breath, we cannot be here. There are two aspects to the air that we breathe.

The first aspect is the chemicals - oxygen, nitrogen, carbon - and they nourish the physical body. The second aspect is the Life Force itself, within the air that we breathe. How much Life Force is circulating has a lot to do with what is going on in our mind, whether there's a lot of chatter going on, whether the mind is quiet, and whether or not we can be in the present moment right here, right now. When Life Force is low, we hang out in the past regretting all the things that went wrong, all the things that we couldn't do, or we're glorifying the past, "Those were the good old days."

If we're not wandering in the past, then we're in the future waiting for our ship to come in. Being right here, right now and accepting what is going on right here and right now is really what allows you to move forward.

William Shakespeare, a great yogi, said through *Hamlet*, "Nothing is good or bad, except the mind makes it so." All the great Masters of the world have said the same.

Being able to look at every situation and ask, "What can I do differently here? What needs to happen now?" requires a calm and steady mind. The more you can be in the present moment, look at things objectively, look at things just as they are, then the better decisions you make so you can move forward. Utilizing the breath is an amazing tool to assist with that.

If you haven't experienced it, skepticism is natural. The ability to harness the secrets of the breath makes a powerful difference. Once you gain that ability, you will have it for a lifetime. It's simple and profound.

Always and everywhere, remember your Self, and don't give up on yourself. Ever.

24. Awaken
Geri Portnoy

Geri Portnoy is the founder of Yoga Del Mar. She holds a Master's degree in International Peace Studies from the University of Notre Dame, is a certified Hatha Yoga teacher, and a Waking Down teacher.

After going through her own dark night of the soul experience and waking up to a non-dual state of oneness, she founded *Yoga of Awakening* – an embodied path of spiritual awakening for the 21st century. Geri helps everyday people who are tired of living a lukewarm life, wake up to engage more intimately with their body, mind, emotions and spirit. Her *Yoga of Awakening* programs help people all over the world awaken to know the freedom of consciousness, the power of authenticity, and the vibrant aliveness of Being. http://yogaofawakening.com

My Vision

As a sensitive child growing up Detroit, Michigan in the sixties I was witness to a time of great unrest, violent upheavals, and a new consciousness coming into the world. People were beginning to stand up for peace, justice, and human rights. Although I was much too young to participate, even as a passive observer, I somehow absorbed those values as a guiding light for my life. Decades later, I was listening to a recording of President Kennedy's speech, I heard him say that the "torch has been passed to a new generation," and I felt like he was talking directly to me. His words unleashed a passionate vision in my heart to help bring peace to our struggling world.

In addition to being deeply aware of the global challenges of our times: war, famine, environmental degradation, and overpopulation, I was also deeply aware of my own internal challenges. In my own heart I felt an unrelenting internal restlessness, discontent, and ennui. Objectively I could see that I had a great life, filled with everything someone my age could want: great friends, a boyfriend I cared about, a beautiful place to live, a career I loved, a family I adored and a lifestyle that brought me joy. At the same time, when I settled down and got quiet, and looked inside, I could feel an ache -- a tightness in my belly that was always there. Like a gemstone with many facets, at times this ache felt like loneliness – a longing for something I could not name, at times it felt like a fundamental depression or an existential anxiety. Whatever facet of expression it took, it felt like "there must be something wrong with me" or "there must be something more to life."

This set up a passionate quest in my life. I was clear that I was here on this planet at this time in history to help relieve the suffering of the world. I was also beginning to see that in order to do that -- to live my vision -- I would also have to find peace in my inner world. And that's when I found the practice of yoga.

At the time, I had just graduated from a Master's Program in International Peace Studies and I was teaching Conflict Resolution and Science at Stevenson Middle School in East Los Angeles. I was a first year teacher and feeling overwhelmed by the amount of papers to grade, the work load of having four different preps, and the monumental task of educating the next generation of students to live, and thrive, in the world.

One of my friends invited me to go to a yoga class on the beach to celebrate Earth Day. I put my towel down on the sand, and we were facing the ocean. I looked out over the ocean and there were some dolphins swimming by in the waves. I closed my eyes. We meditated. We did some yoga. At the end of class, we sang the sound of "om" and when I opened my eyes, the water was sparkling and the dolphins were swimming by again. I felt this unbelievable wave of peace and well-being inside that I hadn't felt in a very long time. It surprised me. I immediately realized that yoga was exactly what my soul needed next. I signed up for classes the very next day and I began a deep and dedicated practice of yoga.

After practicing yoga for several years and discovering a wellspring of inner peace, strength, flexibility, and well being, I realized that teaching yoga was how I could help bring peace to the world. I moved to Del Mar -- a small coastal community in Southern California. And my boyfriend and I opened up a small yoga studio about a mile-and-a-half from the beach called Yoga

Del Mar. I began teaching yoga to people in the local community.

I really felt like I was fulfilling my vision to help relieve the suffering of the world by sharing the practice of yoga with others. I watched people come in with lower back pain and leave class pain-free and happy. As the years passed I saw people become healthier, calmer, stronger, and more peaceful. They told me how much it helped their life and I saw the changes in them. I finally felt like I had fulfilled my vision, but looking back, I can see that was just the start of a much more magnificent journey.

My Voyage

One day during my yoga practice, I was balancing on one arm with my foot behind my head and someone came up to "adjust me." As they lifted my body up it torqued my hip and my back and I heard a crack. Nothing felt the same after that. Something felt "off" in my body and every little movement I made hurt.

My yoga practice – that had brought me so much joy and relief from the discomforts of life -- stopped working for me. It stopped working to lift me up above the discomforts of life, and I began to land more deeply in the reality of my experience -- a reality that included comfortable and uncomfortable feelings. I began to enter into my own "dark night of the soul." There was nothing I could do to get out of it.

Up to this point, my yoga practice had been a reliable way to lift myself "up and out" of my experience and feel better. But during this next period of time, my defenses against feeling the realities of life were beginning to "rot" away. I no longer had the energy to dissociate from feelings I did not want to feel such as my own anger, sadness, and disappointment.

I knew that the word *yoga* meant "connection." I had equated that connection to joining with my breath, the positive sensations in my body, and the feeling of spirit – the transcendent ground of spaciousness and peace. But now, I began to connect to and feel the discomforts of my body, the pain in my hip, the tightness in my back, and the shallowness of my breath.

My first natural impulse was to turn away. To tell you the truth, if I had the capacity to turn away as I had in the past -- ignore the pain or not confront it -- I probably would have. But instead, I found that all my defenses -- all the techniques I had used to distract myself from that kind of deeper pain -- stopped working. In the past, I would have done a two-hour yoga practice or meditated for a half-hour, or maybe done all of that. But now, no matter what I did, there was an inescapable confrontation with the feelings I had previously been avoiding.

To struggle against my own internal experience became more painful that turning toward myself and meeting my own internal experiences. When I felt disappointed because I could not do my regular strong yoga practice, I just let myself feel disappointed. I learned, that it was tolerable to feel disappointed. I began to open up to feel a plethora of emotions that I had never let myself feel before. I came more alive! I felt more courageous, honest, and free to be me.

With the support of a spiritual community called Waking Down, I began to understand that this "dark night of the soul" was actually part of my awakening experience. My old defenses against feeling life fully were falling away and I was opening into greater wholeness. This was huge for me and allowed me to *trust* the experience I was going through, and cooperate with it.

It became a new *samskara* – a new habit – to turn toward myself with curiosity and compassion. To connect more deeply with myself over and over again, when I was frustrated, mad, impatient, joyful, loving, arrogant, selfish, and peaceful. The detached, distant, perspective I had lived in for so long began to collapse in on itself. I came face to face with life, deeply, intimately, meeting each moment exactly as it was.

And then I had my awakening. At the time, I was walking across the room during a workshop. I felt as if I landed in myself. My feet felt like they hit the ground with a "thud." All of the sudden I was "here" in a place of deep connection with all of life. There was no separation. In a way it felt like I had come down out of the bleachers of life and was now in the game of life, *as Life*. I was living in a constant field of non-separation.

I walked outside and felt a seamless continuum with everything. The sun shimmering on the water, the hawk flying across the open sky, branches blowing in the breeze – it was all me. There was no separation. And at the same time, I was also myself, unique and distinct. It was a living paradox of being everything and also being individuated and clearly more "me" than ever before. I no longer felt like something was missing or wrong with me. My quest for wholeness, peace and awakening was over, and my new work in the world was just beginning.

The Value of Lessons Learned

My own awakening experience was the greatest gift of my life. I now know a place of *peace inside me* that's never not there. Whenever I check in, I know myself to be whole, connected to all life, and living in a field of fundamental okay-ness, wellbeing and peace. I also still experience the full spectrum of emotions – all the flavors, all the *rasas* of life, it's just a lot easier because I also experience consciousness – the large spaciousness of being.

Since my awakening I have been helping other people around the world wake up to know who they are. I help them understand that this is a natural part of their maturation as a human being. Historically, it's been the "Holy Grail" of a yoga practice to connect to all parts of oneself including fundamental consciousness -- the place of abiding peace inside. And now it's available to everyday people like you and me.

Here are some of the signs that you might be ready:

1. You start to notice more of your emotional life coming on-line. You feel life more deeply – you might be moved to tears by a beautiful sunset or the words of a sweet poem.

2. You are tired of constantly pushing yourself and running away from the discomfort inside yourself. You are ready to step off the hamster wheel, slow down, and confront what you've been avoiding.

3. You have a longing inside to know who you are, to discover the deep place of peace and well being that is your birthright.

4. You are aware of a fundamental discomfort inside – an

ache, a longing, a gnawing restlessness, a confusing ennui or an existential anxiety that feel like it's "always been there."

I support students in going through this sacred passage to experience their own transition into an embodied spiritual awakening.

Yoga on the mat is just the beginning of the spiritual journey of yoga. Often, initially there is a taste of spiritual awakening – you catch a glimpse of feeling open, spacious, and free. It's something real and it can be an enticement to begin the spiritual quest.

This type of embodied awakening that's happening in the 21st century is about awakening to *both* spiritual spaciousness and one's full humanity. It's a paradoxical experience of being awake as everything and also clearly, distinctively yourself. In this way, one is informed by the totality of spirit and yet moves as an individual with certain gifts and talents to bring to the world.

For me, it's allowed me to discover what my purpose in life is. It's not just to bring peace to people as a momentary fleeting state, instead, it's to help guide people on their own awakening journey into a stage of knowing themselves as the fundamental peace underlying all creation. So they can live from that place of inner connection, blazing their light boldly and brilliantly as a sign post of who we are as human beings.

One of the things I've experienced during my awakening process is how important it is to have other people around you who are also at a similar place in their journey. Part of my vision is to help create these communities, small groups where people can get together and support each other as they go through this process of awakening.

In this awakening process there is a transmission – a collective field of awakening that fuels and propels individual awakening. It's an epigenetic force, a way in which the environment that you are in helps to fuel your own transformational process. You might even feel some of the shifts and changes in your body and in your being right now, just from reading this passage.

You don't have to know how to awaken, in fact you can't. Your mind will want to take over the process, but it doesn't know the way. Like a caterpillar becoming a butterfly, it's programmed into your DNA. They key is being kind to your self. Give yourself permission to feel what you feel and be who you are. Trust in your own process and reach out for help, support and the power of community.

Words of Wisdom and Vision

In order to help people on their journey of awakening I teach a simple three-step process. The fist step is to stop, pause and take a breath. The second step is to drop into your body and feel – feel your breath and whatever other feelings are there. The third step is to connect -- to turn towards your self with love and compassion and meet "what is."

When I practice this on my own, I often add in a *mudra* – a hand gesture. I place my hand over my heart and I do the three-step process:

1. Stop, pause, take a breath
2. Drop into your body
3. Connect to "what is"

This creates a courageous level of intimacy with one's self. A connection to what's unfolding inside. By saying "yes" to one's own inner experience – instead of avoiding, resisting, escaping, or freezing – it allows you to evolve, to grow, to transform and ultimately to awaken.

Yoga has always been a process of connection and a gateway to spiritual awakening. In the past it was just for the few "Olympic type yogis," but today it's available to everyday people like you and I. It is our birthright as human beings to know who we are, to wake up to know the peace and connection that is our very essence. To live without that is to live a life of separation – a life in which it feels like "something is missing," because *it is*.

My vision is to help humanity awaken, so everyone has the opportunity to know who she really is or know who he really is. To evolve and grow in the brilliant light of being – to serve the whole of creation, by being seamlessly connected to everything. To be spiritually awake and living our gifts and talents in life. It is our destiny as a species and it is my great honor to help people move through this sacred transition.

The words of John F. Kennedy still echo in my heart, "the torch has been passed to a new generation . . ." and it is *our* generation, we who now inhabit this Earth. We have this great opportunity to awaken -- to know who we are, to live from a place of peace and connection and creatively move our world forward.

The door is round and open
Don't go back to sleep.
-Rumi

25. Develop Your Humanity
Anne Redelfs, M.D.

Anne Redelfs was born and raised in Beaver, Pennsylvania, a small mill town outside of Pittsburgh. She received a B.A. in Chemistry from Duke University and an M.D. from Tulane University. She trained in both pediatric and psychiatry residencies at Tulane-affiliated hospitals in New Orleans.

Disgruntled by the excessive use of drugs on the mentally ill, she retired from a private practice in psychiatry to pursue independent studies in developmental psychology. She has published her discoveries in a book, *The Awakening Storm*. This is a story about the impact of Hurricane Katrina and the levee disaster on New Orleans and the impact of life's storms and disasters on human beings.

Anne currently conducts a ministry of "listening" and holistic healing in Texarkana, Texas. theawakeningstorm.vpweb.com

My Mission

My vision is to modernize the practice of healthcare. In my lifetime, there have already been many improvements in the field of medicine, such as imaging devices that can make visible every part of our bodies and show its activity level. Robotic surgical procedures are now an option. And scientists are mapping and manipulating genomes with the goal of minimizing genetic disease. These are all extraordinary advancements, yet at the same time, we are still treating our human bodies as less than human. We believe we know how they should be performing, and we attempt to correct them when they aren't performing as we expect. For example, we think our bodies should be healthy, no matter how poorly we eat, how little we sleep, or how much we otherwise stress them. A more evolved practice is to lovingly relate to our bodies – sensing what they need and meeting these needs. I'm not talking about meeting superficial needs, like I'm feeling a need for a double chocolate sundae with extra topping, but meeting the true deeper needs of the body, such as what we need to develop our humanity. To do this, we need to hear each body's human voice, respect the intelligence and care expressed in each symptom we might have, and honor the body's request for change.

Let me explain what I mean by developing our humanity. When we demand human beings act according to strict, externally imposed rules of "good" behaviors, while avoiding equally strict "bad" behaviors, we dehumanize them. We're requiring they behave in a mechanical manner, rather than being true to their human selves or true to a higher spiritual purpose. An example of these rules would be, "Exercise regularly – it is good for your health." Life is too complex for such simple programs to always be effective, in that exercising may be very bad if we are jogging behind moving cars or swimming in a sea of carcinogens. I see this a lot — people following what they've learned is "good." But when they haven't been taught to be equally attentive to their body's perceptions, feelings, and thoughts, they don't apply the information correctly.

So much dehumanizing and secondary harm is perpetrated in our society by these rigid programs as well as the more obvious abuse and neglect of our human needs. To recover, we must seek people who are in touch with their humanity to re-humanize us in each area where our humanness has been deadened or damaged. *Contrary to popular belief, this development is one of our human needs!* Because when we have access to our humanity, including body awareness, a compassionate heart, an open mind, and a conscious spiritual connection through each of these modalities, we can sense when, where, with whom, how, and how much we need to exercise, so that it really is good for us. *And* we exercise our psychological body — the emotional heart and the mind — as much as the physical body. The less access we have to all these components of our humanity, the more likely we are to make mistakes, and the bigger the mistakes we make, such as not listening to our body's human voice.

How I came to my vision. To have a tender and respectful relationship with our bodies is what I learned through my personal and professional experiences with sickness. Each symptom is an indication of a problem, which often includes physical, emotional, and mental components – each aspect of our humanity. To give you a better idea of what I am talking about, let's look at the leading causes of death in our country. Heart disease is first. In our culture, we associate the heart with emotions, such as love. Therefore, incapacitating heart disease is often a manifestation of incapacitating emotional issues. For instance, we may not be circulating our authentic emotions each day and a weak heart is revealing this weakness.

The second most common cause of death in the United States is cancer. Malignant tumors may represent the spread of something in our mind that is contrary to our human life. A preoccupation with image would be an example of this. I go into great detail in my book, *The Awakening Storm*, about how image is created and fed in the average child in our country and how it is maintained in the average adult. So many people live in their imaginations rather than seeing what is truly going on around them and within them *and* within their fellow man.

This is an enormous problem by itself. But also, children need validation, loving support, and guidance in handling their genuine life experiences if they are to mature. When parents live in a fantasy world, an image of what they wished their life had been rather than the truth, they cannot be with their child's genuine experience. They cannot validate and lovingly support the child's legitimate thoughts and feelings about what really happened. And they cannot effectively guide the child. Instead they tend to guide the child into imagery, as they have been guided. They teach a comforting story that the child learns to call reality, while the truth gets stored in the unconscious mind.

Many of our illnesses and injuries are trying to draw our attention to just how debilitating these stories have been to our psychological development. When we are not speaking the truth of our experience, our bodies may fill in the silence with symptoms that reveal the truth. For instance, we may lose our vision if we are blind to this truth. Or we may lose our hearing if we're deaf to the deeper messages of each human voice. Our illnesses and injuries can also be a manifestation of post-traumatic stress disorder, PTSD, which in my opinion, is inevitable when our caretakers are unable to acknowledge and lovingly help us through our greatest traumas.

Part of PTSD is reliving or recreating our traumas, which again can be physical, emotional, or mental. Keeping ourselves stressed is a common example of reliving and recreating an aspect of our traumatic experience. If we've had a traumatic life, we are used to the feeling of being stressed, so we seek out stressful situations, which may include the stress of chronic illness. I'm not suggesting that most people do this consciously; it's usually an unconscious process, particularly when we have a lot of unconscious trauma. Sometimes the very illnesses we succumb to allude to these past traumas, as in sexually abused children having diseases that affect their sexual organs. We may have pain in these areas as reminders of the pain during past trauma or maybe because we are feeling guilty and are unconsciously punishing these parts of us with pain. Or perhaps we choose a painful, disabling treatment to do the punishing. There are many possibilities of what our bodies are trying to help us work through by our various symptoms and disease processes *and* through our choices of treatment.

My Voyage

My professional journey started in pediatrics during my two-year residency with Tulane-affiliated hospitals and clinics in New Orleans. While I was learning primarily the biological causes of the children's illnesses, I found my curiosity growing in regards to the psychological causes. To me, the emotional and mental components in disease processes were just as important as the physical components, and these psychological components were always present, whether the illness was diagnosed as psychosomatic or not. I remember asking the sick children in the hospital wards, "Why are you sick?" and then I would listen intently for the answer. Sooner or later, they let me know. There was always an intelligent reason, and often the cause included others. For instance, one boy had a father who was lost in the fast lane of a high-powered job, and the boy's devastating disease got dad to slow down and adjust his priorities. This boy was willing to forfeit his physical life in order to save the psychological life of his father. A girl who was hospitalized with recurring symptoms just wanted to bring her divorced parents back together. Their visits to the hospital because of her illness were the only times they were in each other's company for more than a few minutes. So our illnesses are requests for correction, inside ourselves and outside ourselves, in those we're closest to. They challenge us to develop ourselves and each other in some profound way.

One of the challenges for me has been to share this information about psychological causes of illness when people often have strong reactions. To give you an example, some people react to this information as if I am trying to hurt them. This makes sense in that when we have hidden our hurts in our unconscious mind and clung to a fantasy instead of reality, those who refer to the truth of our experience can *seem* hurtful.

Thus, the very situation we needed as children, people validating and supporting our genuine experience, now seems frightening. It threatens to bring up all the pain we have denied and repressed over the years. Yet when we run away from this pain and the people who refer to it, we curtail our development. On top of the pain and the fear of it surfacing, we then also have a lot of guilt for avoiding what we need to grow. When I share with people what their bodies may be communicating, this guilt often surfaces as well. They feel guilty too because if they had had this information sooner, they or their loved ones might not have suffered to such a degree and maybe some wouldn't have prematurely died!

I think it is important that we extend the same graciousness to ourselves that we do our developing children. Just as kids follow a certain path in their physical development, we all have a predictable path of psychological development. Blaming ourselves for taking so much time to mature is like blaming a child for taking nearly two decades before being ready to leave his family of origin. Maturation takes time—individually and collectively.

We have to progress from a history-based perspective to a new paradigm. Consider for a moment the many children and adults who suffered and died from infectious diseases before antibiotics. For instance, penicillin was discovered by Alexander Fleming in 1928, and then used clinically in the 40s. Historically, opening up to new information and the effective implementation of that information takes a certain amount of time and adjustment. When penicillin became available, we had to leap from an experience-based perspective of bacterial infections causing many fatalities to embrace the possibility that antibiotics can kill bacteria and prolong life. Thankfully we made this leap, and people now routinely recover from infectious diseases that were typically fatal 100 years ago. This new paradigm of listening to the requests for change in our body symptoms requires the same leap of faith. When we make this leap, I believe the number of recoveries will be similarly impressive.

The triumphs of this philosophy and practice would be the surmounting of all forms of illness and injury the more that we listen to the communications in each symptom, investigate the emotional and mental causes equally to the physical causes, and respond to the requests for change that our physical and psychological bodies are asking from us. *Our Spirit is asking a lot too!* I have seen miraculous healings when people make the choice to deeply listen and appropriately respond. I remember one adolescent, for example, who had severe food allergies, which resulted in her having a thin, sickly appearance. I persistently inquired why her body was rejecting these foods, and she eventually recalled that the rejection began after having a horrible argument at the dinner table with her controlling mother, the cook in the family. She hated her mom in that moment, but she didn't feel right about hating her mom, so she instead hated everything on the table and could not stomach any of those foods again. This girl went into therapy to work on her anger toward her mother, and she returned to a normal diet without any further allergic reactions.

This misplaced anger is such a common cause of illness. In my opinion, investigating anger should be part of every interview a doctor conducts, but usually the physical body gets the most focus. I believe our cultural focus on the physical body more than the psychological, is one of the main causes of our illnesses. The sick body is lovingly amplifying the suffering of our deprived and abused hearts and minds that we may acknowledge and treat it, but how often do we listen? Several doctors challenged some people I knew to look inward and make a few changes as a remedy for their rapidly deteriorating physical health. These patients responded with, "I would rather die!" Their honesty was evidenced by their deaths shortly after. To me, this was tragic!

The Value of Lessons Learned

Once we understand that we are not innocent victims of our accidents and illnesses, but are participants in bringing about these intelligent communications, we can apply this message anywhere in our lives. Whatever is going on, no matter how disastrous or seemingly outside of our control, we can look at it as mirroring something about our own psychology. A traumatic event in the present may reflect dynamics from our past, which require more *human* involvement. It may be helping us overcome a weakness or teaching us valuable skills that we currently need to acquire. It may be preparing us for a future that we have yet to envision, let alone set goals and objectives. There are so many possibilities beyond: "This should not be happening!" "I don't want this!" And then seeking out people or God Himself to make it stop. In all circumstances lie many developmental opportunities.

Words of Wisdom and Vision

As we go about our busy lives, we need to notice what our bodies are contributing in the way of expert insight. The more we do this, the more we see just how much assistance is coming to us for our life's journey, and not just from people, but from situations. I recommend pausing frequently as you go about each day and prayerfully asking what any person or situation is showing you about yourself and your voyage. Was he, she, or it offering some practical guidance, encouraging some much needed abilities, or aiding you in becoming aware of and overcoming some shortcoming? The more we listen deeply to our symptoms and circumstances, the more we realize that there is indeed *Someone* out there — Our Divine Doctor. The more we look to Him, the more He gives us a vision of what our lives are to be and how to get there. The more we feel His Presence, the more we come to understand that He is employing the vehicle of our lives to communicate with every one of us. And He is employing this vehicle to move us to mature every one of us…and every part of us…until we are all holy and wholly like Him.

Voyage to Spirituality and Fulfillment

26. Follow Your Transformational Path
Louise M. Finlayson, Ph.D.

Louise Finlayson grew up in a blue-collar family and neighborhood outside of Buffalo, New York. Not only did she graduate from high school and college with honors, but went on to graduate school where she earned a Ph.D. in clinical psychology.

While at Harvard Medical School, she was invited to join the faculty, but that is not the path she chose. Instead, she has nurtured, cultivated, and shared her gifts in her 30 years as a clinical psychologist in private practice, in 15 years as a transformational coach and motivational speaker and a 25-year yoga meditation practice and other expansive personal growth programs. www.louisefinlayson.com

My Vision

I came to my vision from a place of not knowing when I was young, but, in fact, over the years coming to find out that I was really very close to Spirit—throughout my young life, and now through my whole adult life, knowing things on some level other people didn't, and not knowing that I knew that.

I was connected to a sense of purpose from a young age. I didn't understand that other people didn't experience their lives that way. I was unaware that I could see the bigger picture in a way that other people usually couldn't. I now understand the uniqueness of my gift. I have spent most of my adult life honing skills and practices that support me helping others skillfully using my gifts.

My Voyage

I was invited to join the faculty of Harvard Medical School. I turned that opportunity down in order to develop a private practice where I have really close contact with my clients. I came to the decision like many decisions in my life; I didn't always know why I was doing what I was doing in the moment.

In retrospect, I see why that was such an important decision in my life. In the moment, I made it for reasons of lifestyle and saying that I really wanted to be able to focus on my marriage and on having a family, and not really wanting to live in an urban environment. I made the decision based on what seemed like maybe small things, but it turned out that these were really very important things in terms of what was necessary for me to live a fulfilled life.

It's so easy to do what people expect or do what looks like the logical thing, and we lose our soul in a way from that place. We lose our path and our way for ourselves, because expectations are really external kinds of things, and they don't have a lot to do with us.

I would say there was struggle in my decision, absolutely. Part of my ego was saying, "Yes!" I was not just blue-collar – I was a no collar family growing up, and I put myself through all this schooling. My family did not support me. It was like, "Wow! I've reached a pinnacle here!"

Yet on the other side of it, there was a part of me saying, "Yes, but I feel like there's some way that this isn't really my path." I was in this place of one foot straddling into this world and my other foot straddling into the other world, and then having to make a decision. What's really true for me? My ego was really battling me on that one.

I'm happy with my decision, and sometimes I say, "Oh gee, what did I do?" Sometimes I still to this day say, "What? I could have had that!" Yet, in my truest heart of hearts, I know that that would not have been a path of happiness for me.

It's a highly competitive world. I love to compete for fun, but I don't like to compete on a day-to-day basis. I'm a tennis player and I like competing that way, and I don't really compete against my opponents. I compete against my last best game. For me, that's fun. I don't want to necessarily live my life in a competitive environment, and that's what it would have been like for me. I think that would have been a source of enormous stress.

I never had a challenge opening up my private practice. I had this odd phenomenon where I was invited to rent some space from somebody who was a psychiatrist. He said, "You'll do fine." He referred one or two patients to me. It seemed magical, that from then on I had more clients calling me than I ever could see. It was a very wonderful experience to start a business and never have to advertise or be wondering where the next client was coming from. I was very fortunate that way.

Then I studied coaching and began to add coaching as a service I offered. Coaching was not really a phenomenon that was known in my area when I started, so that was a little bit more of a stretch for me in terms of developing the marketing of my coaching practice.

That's been an ongoing learning experience for me, and I feel much more comfortable with it now than I did way back when. Now I don't have to explain what a coach is anymore, whereas when I first became a coach, people in the Northeast were not particularly aware of what that was.

A lot of times in my psychotherapy practice, I will coach my clients as well as use psychotherapy. Say if I have a deep trauma client, I'll work on the trauma and help that person get past living like a victim. The psychotherapy process allows for transformation on a very deep level — changing the way a person thinks, sees the world, and behaves. Once the trauma patient works through the trauma and is no longer living life from a victim-stance, then coaching helps with restructuring the person's life, from reactive to proactive.

I use a coaching model to help the client envision what he or she really wants to manifest in his or her life. If somebody comes to me deeply depressed, I will work with them to transform the way that they're thinking and therefore how they feel, how they see things, and the stories that they tell themselves. That's the psychotherapy part. Once they have that transformation, they say, "Now that I'm no longer thinking like a depressed person, what kind of life do I want to live?" Then coaching allows them to be able to see the big picture, to think out of the box, and to see possibilities they weren't able to see before.

The Value of Lessons Learned

There was a woman that I worked with who had what I would call it torture in her childhood. From almost birth on through the age of 13 or 14, she experienced a very high level of very sadistic behavior directed towards her. Since adolescence, pretty much every day of her life she had thought about committing suicide and had made many suicide attempts. She had been in and out of psychiatric hospitals and had been through many, many therapists over many years. She never felt better. She was chronically suicidal and was under-functioning in her life.

When she found me, she was not in great shape. We worked very intensively for three years. We restructured the way she saw everything in her life. We used spiritual and psychological principles to help her reconstruct the way she felt about herself, the way she felt about the external world, and then she started to function much better. She started to bloom, and we then began to look towards the future and what she wanted.

She has now highly functional and contributes in many ways. She is an accomplished singer and sings professionally now. She's also an accomplished photographer and sells her photography. She has also become a spiritual counselor and helps other people who feel suicidal. She is just contributing to the world in spades. I feel deeply gratified when I think about the outcome of our work together.

I see that when we have a spiritual basis for our life and we see the connectedness of everything — that we're all connected, that we're all one, that there is no separation — then things begin to really shift and morph for us. When we believe what we think, we end up getting into trouble. We get very involved in our stories and our thoughts, which are created by our pain or created by our ego. It also gets us in trouble when we seek immediate gratification. I help my clients understand the principle of connection – there's nothing other than love.

This can be hard to grasp when you've had your struggles. I've had my struggles in my own life growing up, and anything that I teach has come from me living these things. That's why I teach from a place of knowing, not from a place of having learned it in a book. My idea is to help people be liberated from their self-limiting beliefs, from their stories, and from their ego structures. Not that we're ever free of our ego, but to be able to use our ego appropriately, not to have the ego running the show all the time.

I like to leave my clients with an understanding of universal principles and tools to apply them. I will be at a movie theater or someplace, and run into one of my former clients, and they'll be with a friend. They will say, "This is Louise. I've worked with her." The friend whom I've never met will say, "You're Louise? I've learned so much from you," because my client taught them what they learned. That's like the pebble in the pond effect – the ripple effect. I teach people real spiritual skills that are so tangible that they can be transmitted from my clients to their families, to their friends and those people can transmit those to their friends and family – I see that as a ripple effect.

Words of Wisdom and Vision

When making a decision, it helps to quiet the voices of the nay-sayers within and without. While it is important to assess risk, letting risk aversion determine our decisions ends up meaning that we end up playing small. Learning how to really get quiet, through mindfulness, meditation, or some other method of quieting the mind and opening to Spirit. It's helpful to be able to know when you're in connection with yourself, when you're in flow, when Spirit is moving through you versus when it's the ego driving you to move to a certain thing because the ego wants some gratification. Understanding that difference is really important.

Once you're there, you become liberated. You become free to really listen to Spirit. This path requires courage. We think this is all going to be light and airy – but this path takes true grit. It takes devotion, practice, the ability to do things that seem scary on the surface, and underneath it, believe that it's all okay, that it's all in service of love. There is no such thing as failure. The ego won't believe that. We will experience doubt. That's when maintaining your practice and connecting with other people who are also moving in the realm of spirit can be very helpful.

When we're the lone voice out there in the wilderness, it can feel pretty lonely, especially when other people are saying, "Don't leave your job. How could you leave that relationship? How could you start that business?" or whatever the thing is.

Learning how to really listen inside and then also know that the worst possible thing that can happen isn't so bad.

There are no problems. Each step that we take the Universe will give us feedback; we can learn from the feedback and evolve or we can keep doing the same thing over and over again, ignoring feedback. The Universe is impartial that way. It is reliable about feedback. We can listen and learn, and or stay stuck.

The biggest help for me is getting into nature or meditating, and both are really great when I can do that, because it's the slowing down rather than speeding up. One of the things I notice is that when I'm out of touch with myself, I tend to speed up. My go-to place then is to slow down, make fewer decisions rather than more decisions, and find space to meditate and to connect with nature, because that's where my source is.

27. No Excuses
Drew Hunthausen

As an 11-year-old, **Drew Hunthausen** lay unresponsive in a coma day after day; the doctors didn't hold out much hope. At one time about 10 days into his illness, Drew's family was informed that he would likely die or be a vegetable on a feeding tube. They didn't think he would make it through the next couple days.

However, it is clear that God's plan for Drew on this earth was not complete. After enduring a torturous three-month coma brought on by bacterial meningitis, he began to wake up, only to find he had lost his eyesight and much of his hearing. The resulting journey would be one filled with very significant challenges.

Today, as an adult who has graduated from college with a

degree in Sociology, Drew wakes up each morning with a different kind of vision. He delivers a message of hope and encouragement, and that anything is possible! You will no doubt walk away with a renewed sense of purpose and meaning for life after hearing Drew share his remarkable story. www.DrewsInspirations.com

My Vision

I am blind and hearing impaired, having lost these senses after contracting bacterial meningitis in 1998 when I was 11 years old. I came home from the hospital unable to even sit up, much less stand or walk. The road to recovery has been a long and challenging journey through which I have learned to meet life's challenges with hope and optimism. I wake up each morning with a different kind of vision, one that is much richer and more defined than mere eyesight. It is a vision that is comprised of faith, hope, and the desire to accomplish all that God has created me to be and do.

We all have a choice to make each day… whether to focus on what we have lost, don't have, or wish we had, or to focus on what we are grateful for, the blessings in our lives. I encourage you to practice this "attitude of gratitude." For when we consistently do so, powerful things happen that change who we are and how we live!

Since graduating from college, where I had a constant goal and something to work on every day, the resulting journey to determine what I was going to do with the rest of my life was, for a time, extremely frustrating. We all have struggles and hardships to deal with, but mine were a little unique. I would think to myself, "What can a blind and hearing impaired person do with his life? How can I contribute? How can I support myself? What really do I have to offer?" During this time, numerous job applications went unanswered.

Through the years, one thing I have learned is that you can never give up. No matter what our definition of God is, He has a special plan for each of us in this world. We just need to find it!

Living in gratitude with a positive attitude and eliminating the excuses, opens us up to identifying our passions and dreams. We learn what we are gifted at and are inspired to action in pursuing those dreams. Deep down we all want to be all that we were born to be, but most of us lack both the vision and the faith. The good news is that we can find the vision and develop the faith when we learn to live a life of "attitude, gratitude, and no excuses!" Come on a journey with me to learn how.

My Voyage

We each have our own unique journey in life. Being successful is not just about reaching the goal; it is mostly about the journey.

Finally home from the hospital after 5 long months, I was blind with no hearing in my left ear and a partial loss in my right. I was so weak that I needed help just to sit up. The question of what would I do with my life was not yet on my radar screen. Life was filled with physical therapy, home schooling, and longing for the life I had lost. It was almost impossible to think of myself as the same person I was 5 months previous before all this craziness, but at the core, I was! I slowly regained my strength both physically, as well as mentally and emotionally.

For the time being, I convinced myself that my current condition was temporary and that the "real" Drew would be back!

After being home schooled for the 7th grade year, I had regained enough strength to mostly ditch my wheelchair at the beginning of 8th grade. This meant I could return to campus with my friends! The newfound freedom from my wheelchair was paired with the ability to eat more normally as my stomach was not quite as fragile (I had ruptured a bowel and underwent a subsequent bowel resection while in the hospital where I lost about 18 inches of my colon).

This bitter sweet revelation was very exciting at first, but since I wasn't getting much exercise at all, I soon gained a lot of weight, going from a very skinny and weak 96 pounds, to a hefty 175 lbs. I did gain quite a bit of muscle as I got stronger, but not nearly enough to match this crazy gain. Unfortunately, that trend continued as I grew older and I struggled with weight for many years.

While the high school years were challenging on all fronts, I had my family and many wonderful folks help me get through it. My biggest take away involves sports. I had been a pretty fair baseball player and golfer prior to getting sick. Now there was seemingly nothing I could do… until I discovered that I could learn to like swimming! The swim team embraced my presence during sophomore season and, while I was anything but fast, I was on the team. That was huge for me and I will forever be grateful. The swim team was the first thing for me that was not defined by my disabilities, but by my abilities! Today I am in training to be an open water ocean swimmer!

I pushed on through junior college and university at California State University Long Beach, where they have an excellent disabled students support system. Even so, college is a time where you must learn to advocate for yourself as you navigate the many challenges encountered. I had to arrange for my own note-takers, campus guides, and drivers each semester. Sometimes I was fortunate to have a person carry over to a new semester, but most often new people had to be found. Effectively navigating the disabled student services was a process all by itself. I attained great personal growth during those college years. Given all the challenges, I'm very proud of my Sociology degree.

My weight ultimately reached about 215 lbs. In February of 2013, I decided I needed to do something about it. Through a combination of healthy eating and exercise, I managed to lose 46 pounds over about 5 months. I am proud of the discipline I had to employ to achieve this goal. I can't even begin to explain the positive difference in how I feel, both physically and emotionally. While I can't see myself, the feedback from others in how I look has also been very positive. The doctors tell me that science has a decent chance of someday restoring my vision. As you might guess, I am most interested in finding out what I look like. For now, I am thankful to be unencumbered by physical appearance in others, as my vision goes straight to the heart. You are all beautiful!

I am called a "miracle" by my parents and those who were part of my life when I got sick. All things considered that is true no doubt, but the journey through adolescence and young adulthood didn't always feel miraculous. I struggled day in and day out to muster the energy for school, physical therapy, and whatever else life threw at me. During these years, thoughts of my future were often frustrating, as I had no idea what I would be able to do, and certainly had no clear picture of what God's plan would be for my life. The focus on school allowed me to avoid focusing on what I had lost and what I would be able to realistically do in the future. It is clear to me now that I was also surrounded by God's grace and those who loved me.

During school, I had some opportunities to speak and realized I was relatively good at it and enjoyed it. However, I still did not clearly see the vision that would bring me to where I am today. After graduation, through a series of events, conversations, and reading, I began to discover that I had a gift for inspiring and motivating others through telling my unique story. Remarkably, the tragedy of my illness was being transformed into something positive to share with the world! Now as an inspirational speaker and author, I am both excited and motivated to move forward across the world and touch as many people as possible with my story and message of "attitude, gratitude, and no excuses!"

My journey through life since my illness is driven from the vision I have to be the most and the best I can be, and through my message, to empower and encourage others to do the same!

The Value of Your Lessons Learned

As you experience challenges, you become stronger and learn lessons of immeasurable value.

The lessons learned during my journey into adulthood are summed up in the motto I strive to live by on a daily basis, "Attitude, gratitude, and no excuses!" We must make a decision when we wake up each morning of what kind of a day we want to have. It is our choice. Most folks don't know or believe this to be true, but it is. We can make that choice for ourselves each and every day.

People often think to themselves that others just don't understand how it really is for them, how difficult things are. They mistakenly view most other folk's lives as being better or easier than theirs. To some degree, we all probably do a little of this; but the truth is, we all have difficult "stuff" in our lives.

Sometimes it is there for reasons out of our control – like maybe we contracted bacterial meningitis and lost our vision and much of our hearing. Sometimes it is there as a consequence of bad decisions we have made maybe with our finances or in our personal lives. Whether our own fault or not, after a while, we develop a habit of what Zig Ziglar used to call, "stinkin thinkin."

"Stinkin thinkin" involves focusing on our problems and making excuses that keep us from being truly joyful and living in gratitude. Here is a personal example. I am a very social person who loves people, especially my family and friends. If I let myself focus on the fact that my sister Chelsea, who I love to hang with, now lives in Montana and my brother Scott in Huston, and that friends don't really call or seek me out nearly as much as I would like for reasons out of my control, it would tend to make me feel sad, lower my healthy vibration, and decrease my chances of a joyful and productive day. That's when Zig would say we are suffering from "hardening of the attitudes," and need a "check-up from the neck up."

I have learned there is a better way and that we can provide our own check-up from the neck up. I can acknowledge the feelings and then choose to focus on how grateful I am for a loving sister and brother. I can remember the new friends and good people God sends my way every day and reach out to one or two on Facebook, with a phone call, or via email. I can think of those I have recently come in contact with who need my encouragement and pass some along to them. God has thus made me into a messenger of good will and he rewards me with a joyful soul. He will reward you too!

It is also true that I would never choose to have lost my eyesight and much of my hearing. This circumstance has brought upon me many unforeseen challenges. While no one in their right mind would have chosen these challenges, without them, I would not be writing these words. I would not have had the opportunities and experiences that have lead me to where I am today — positively impacting people's lives. I know I will continue to face many more challenges on my journey as an inspirational speaker, but am encouraged to know that I will be impacting lives for the better.

What we learn is that when we are living in that healthy zone of "attitude, gratitude, and no excuses," we attract all manner of positive people and opportunities. This is called the law of attraction. In simple terms, you attract and get what you put out into the world, including your thoughts, actions, words, and intentions. It's truly amazing how this really works in everyday life. Concurrently, God tells us in the Scriptures (I am paraphrasing from no particular translation) that our faith can move mountains; to focus on the good; that whatever good thing we ask in faith, He wants to give us; and that, if we keep our eyes on Him, all things will work together for the good. No matter which example resonates with you – law of attraction or the Scriptures, it is clear that what we lend our energy to and focus on, definitely matters!

As we practice and learn to focus on what we are grateful for, life's challenges don't go away. We just learn to navigate the challenging waters with greater ease and with a joyful heart. Our attitude naturally turns positive and the "excuses" diminish.

Probably the most important lesson I've learned for life in general, no matter if we have a disability or not, is that we can't be the best at everything. We are gifted in some areas and not in others. We can't all be professional golfers, great musicians, or financial gurus. We can, however, learn to identify our gifts and our limitations and then be the best we can be. Learning to accept that as enough is huge. Don't make excuses, be grateful for the gifts you have and put yourself out there to achieve your all! Be bold and face your fears with the confidence that you have what it takes!

We are all a work in progress. My intention and sincere desire is to help each and every one of you be all you can be by living a "no excuses" life filled with gratitude!

Words of Wisdom and Vision

Here are three concrete and important ways to help you in your journey to your vision.

1. Be Intentional - A few years ago, my dad taught me something he called the 10-10 exercise. He had learned it from a coach he once had, and practicing it really has made a difference in my life. Here is how it works.

Have an intention each morning to take 15-20 minutes and sit down with a notebook. Make two columns and label one "Grateful/Blessings", and the other "Desires/Prayers".

Now write down 10 things you are grateful for or that you consider blessings in your life. These could be things like your spouse or girlfriend/boyfriend, your kids or siblings, your job, a certain friend or friends, a pleasant encounter you had yesterday, your health, a beautiful day, your pet, good news of any kind, etc. Write down things from the most insignificant to very significant. Try to identify some new things to be grateful for each day, but it is ok to keep writing down some of the same things. The important thing is to write them down anew every day.

In the other column, write down 10 things you would like to have or accomplish or that you are praying for. These could be things like schedule one new speaking gig this week, improved health for yourself, a friend or loved one, a grateful heart, improved communication with a spouse or a friend, that a door would open for that new job (perhaps that you would be attracted to just the right people to open that door), that you would be a blessing to all you meet today, and whatever else you can think of, no matter how big or small.

What this simple exercise does it create an intentional focus on both being grateful and on what you want more of in your life. Follow it for 30 days and see for yourself. You will notice things start to change in your life because of how you are changing your focus.

2. Take care of yourself physically – develop a regular habit of exercise. It seems like everyone likes to tell you this but we see a minority of people actually follow a regular schedule of exercise. Perhaps, if I tell you what I go through to exercise, you will be motivated to set up a program for yourself.

I do belong to a club but can't really go there and navigate the club on my own. Therefore, I had to go in and speak with the manager to ask if they would work with me to navigate between pieces of equipment. This is a bit unusual but he said yes. They would work it out. So now I either get a ride there or call the Disabled bus service to pick me up and take me. Then I must have the disabled bus service take me home. I can wait up to an extra 30 minutes on either end for the ride, and have sat on the bus for up to an hour while they dropped others off first. Still, I am grateful that I can get to the gym at all. While at the gym, I keep my phone with me and call the front desk when I need to move to another piece of equipment. It is a little inconvenient, but in the end, I can get a good workout.

The truth is that we don't really need a gym to have a decent workout. A walking program and a few exercises at home on the family room carpet can go a long way. Cycling is an excellent form of exercise as well. My dad and I have done some tandem riding and enjoy it a lot. He's the captain and I'm the blind stoker on the back seat. I'm actually looking for a new captain, as the old man isn't quite what he used to be.

I also swim regularly in our pool at home and am in the process of organizing some support and help to begin training for open water ocean swimming. Unfortunately none of it, save the swimming at home in my own pool, are exercise practices I can do on my own. Nonetheless, I remain grateful for the help and that I can still do them.

Regular exercise improves both our physical and our emotional selves. Aerobic activity done for 30 minutes or more actually has been shown to create an endorphin response (feel good brain chemicals) that is quite nice. Runners call it the "runner's high" but you don't necessarily need to be running to experience some of it.

3. Know that we don't navigate through life alone. Whether we are fully able bodied or disabled in some significant way, we get by with the help of our friends, family, co-workers, and sometimes total strangers. Be intentional about helping others, and learn to be humble and accept the graciousness and charity of those choosing to help you when you need it. Another saying from Zig Ziglar (he was a favorite of my dad's) goes something like this, "If you help enough other people get what they want, you will get what you want."

Here are some additional short thoughts to help you on your journey:

Always be Truthful.

Always keep promises and commitments.

Humor is essential.

Look for the positive in everyone and in everything you do.

Understanding must come before being understood.

Enjoy the beauty of God's natural creations.

Have faith and seek guidance and wisdom from your higher power (to me that is the one God who created the universe and sent His only son to save us – love to talk about Him with you anytime).

Be true to your heart.

Set goals and follow through to achievement them.

Give thanks and praise God for what you have and who you are.

Relax and take vacations as frequently as you can, even just mini vacations, if that is all you can manage.

Surround yourself with loving and supportive people.

Speak and Act from your heart.

Live in the present.

Life is an attitude.

Love and accept others just how they are; try not to judge.

Enjoy and have fun with life!

28. Unite for Success
Sabrina Williams

Sabrina Williams is a Bestseller Author and she has diversified finance and business experience as a licensed Mortgage Broker, a licensed Insurance Agent, Project Manager, Real Estate Manager, HBB Owner and she is a National Media Branding Consultant along with being a member of the Legacy 360 Dream Team.

She began to write books as a platform to raise awareness that will bring about unity and raise funds for a pilot program that will assist in improving the quality of life and the lives of loved ones.

Her plans are to Petition the President of America to meet with the legacy 360 Dream Team in person to discuss an anticipated Nobel Prize winning Concept that will bring about an epic change!

Help her to make the world a better place by signing her petition, buying a book and spreading the word. sabrinatheauthor.com

My Vision

The Legacy 360 Dream Team consists of members who have collaborated together to provide solutions that will eliminate a lot of our country's debt and problems that a lot of families are facing today due to our economic crisis. That's a little snippet of what the Legacy 360 Dream Team does.

We're planning on eliminating our country's debt as I previously stated, providing education without the burden of debt, and eliminating or reducing poverty by 25% to 75%. We're planning on reducing the obesity epidemic, saving our Social Security retirement program, and circumventing the loss of 401Ks. We're reducing the need of government subsidies, and we're also planning to restore the American dream of home ownership and prevent foreclosure, and much, much more.

We'll be reaching out to a lot of the parents and teachers, principals, ministers, active service members, police officers, firemen, community leaders, celebrity and radio and TV personalities in an effort to unify our country and get assistance in obtaining the necessary services needed to achieve this goal. It is a known fact that when our government is divided, the country suffers greatly, but when our parents, teachers, principals, and ministers are divided, it turns our children's lives upside down, and their future is laced with potential failure.

My Voyage

I am the mother of four wonderful, beautiful children. I'm also the coauthor of the bestseller *The Art and Science of Success, Volume II*. I also will be releasing two more books soon. The titles are: *Sabrina's Inspirational Quotes* and *Media Marketing Branding Tips by Sabrina*. I have diverse finance and business experience as a licensed mortgage broker, a licensed insurance agent, project manager, real estate manager, and now consultant along with the members of the Legacy 360 Dream Team.

First and foremost, I am a Matthew:25 Christian – "In all that I am or ever will be, I owe to my Heavenly Father and my Savior, Jesus Christ."

In all my endeavors, I strive for success. I met a minister who loves teaching God's word and saving souls, and he taught me that Christianity is not just about telling people about Christ, but is also about helping them with their daily problems.

For example, if you're a man or a woman whose lights are about to be turned off or facing eviction and you go and sit and try and teach them about what Jesus says, it's going to be hard because their mind will be so focused on their lights about to be shut off or that they're about to get evicted.

As we know, Jesus fed the hungry, he healed the sick – he helped them first with their earthly needs before he taught them the gospel. Like Jesus, my purpose in life is to improve the quality of life for families around the world.

The Value of Lessons Learned

As a young, vulnerable child, I was molested and physically abused by people who I thought loved and cared for me. I cried for many years during that period. I ended up running away from home. I eventually dropped out of school. Also, at the age of 14, I was shot in the head as a result of an accident.

Many, many years later I was able to overcome that, and I later married and my four beautiful children were born. I had many sleepless nights during my marriage, not knowing whether or not my kids and I would have a place to live, because we were constantly being faced with being evicted from our home. A lot of the evictions came as a result of my husband's misuse of money, his gambling problems, and him just not being able to sustain a job because of his inappropriate actions on the job and constantly being late for work.

Besides all of that, that was not my only worry. I was once on government housing. There were times when we had next to nothing to eat in the house. I fed my children and my husband what was there in the house at that time. As for myself, I don't know if you know what flour bread is, but it's just simply taking flour and water and mixing it together and cooking it on your stovetop, and that was my meal.

I can reflect back on locking myself in the bathroom and crying my eyes out one school year because my husband wasn't going to be able to purchase school clothing for my children, again because of his misuse of money.

I ended up turning to a friend for help. I decided one day enough was enough. I went out, I got a job, and I moved myself and my kids out of that situation. I later went back to school and I earned my high school diploma. I became a licensed insurance agent for one of the largest insurance agencies in the country.

After being in the business of selling insurance, I decided I needed something more challenging. I got with a fellow member of the church, and we decided to partner with this company and go into business together. Our new business partner made a lot of promises regarding the day-to-day business dealings, along with other promises. In order to make the business really flourish, we sometimes worked 12 to 16 hour shifts each in the belief that the company would make good on its promises.

After a period of time, we came to realize that the company was not going to make good on what they promised, and the company was using us for their own gain. Now, with all that I had been through, I could have easily tucked my tail between my legs and cried and ran off, but that's not what I'm made of. I'm always reminded that if I could survive being molested, which is far more tragic, then I can survive whatever obstacle is thrown my way.

What I've learned is that it is through overcoming great trials and tribulations that God enables us to become great leaders. It was through my pain and suffering that motivated me to work to achieve more in life, both for me and for my children. It was the lack of parenthood that was denied to me when I was younger, the division that separated my family, and the absence of a legacy that I should have been left with that inspired me to anticipate a Nobel Prize with a concept that will again reverse the obesity epidemic, drastically reduce poverty, reduce the need of government subsidy, restore the American dream of home ownership, provide employment, prevent foreclosures, and eliminate our country's debt. I also envision decreasing the crime rate, assist with resolving our Social Security problems, and leave a legacy that will change the world.

In my humble opinion, I believe that true success is composed of many elements, levels, and parts. Each are entwined or should lock together in order to achieve higher levels of success. To me, true success is not measured by whether you have a big home, how expensive your car is, or the amount of money you have in your bank – nor is it measured by your level of social status. It is measured by overcoming life's obstacles.

Words of Wisdom and Vision

I would like to encourage those out there to set goals, take it one day at a time, stay on the path regardless of life's obstacles, consider each step you take an accomplishment, and remember that the more steps you take, the more accomplished you will become.

I would like to see stability in the home where there is no worrying about, "How am I going to pay for my child's education? How I am going to pay the next month's rent?" I just want to see unity in families, united as one.

I would say a tip for success in life is to commit to a belief system that is greater than you, and to commit to a system that teaches against selfishness. The idea of being successful in your personal life or in your business endeavors without removing selfishness is an illusion. The vision is a clear pathway to failure, and it will hinder what you seek to accomplish. Unity is the foundation for success, and it will never let you fail.

29. Make a Difference
Lauren Perotti

Lauren Perotti delivered her first keynote talk as a valedictorian of her 1968 graduating class, Catholic Kindergarten. This lady started very young. With sparkle and humor, Lauren has delivered messages of leadership, inspiration, and of what it takes to triumph in the ABCs of life on many stages and pages in years since.

She is a coauthor of the book, *God Allows U-Turns,* and is working on her book, *Destiny by Divine Design.* Blending 30 years of unique expertise in business, psychology, and the arts, Lauren helps spiritual seekers, who want to make a big difference in the world, to reignite their passion, get a clear vision of their purpose and the next direction, shift limiting blocks, and create an action plan so they can start moving toward their goals. www.laurenperotti.com

My Vision

I'm a passionate person and have many passions. One of my greatest passions – you can probably even say my mission in life – is to help visionaries who not only want to make a bigger difference in the world, but in their own lives. I'm talking about any of you who may be feeling disconnected from your fire inside, because I've been there. I can help you discover, design, live and lead your Soul-centered life and livelihood with more passion, play and true prosperity.

I really believe that each one of us is alive and here to express and live a unique purpose. I've discovered that I'm here to help light people up; we light up when we're connected to our Soul purpose.

I've travelled a long and winding road to discover and get clear about my vision. As a child, I learned to look for the light as a way to overcome my fear of the dark. One of my most potent sources of light was and still is my connection with the world of Spirit – God, the angels and other aspects of the Divine. On a more literal level, I came to my life's purpose through many personal development tools, programs, and practices I have studied and cultivated over the last 25 years. I'm talking about psychotherapy, personality profiling systems, my Master's degree program in psychology and expressive arts therapy, life purpose hand analysis, and more. I'm a seeker, a quester. I love to explore all these fascinating perspectives, and I love to share their wisdom.

My Voyage

I've had many significant trials and challenges to overcome

throughout my life's journey. Yet I've always had a can-do spirit, which is partly innate to my Italian heritage nature, and partly nurture. Instead of allowing these trials to derail my life, I was open to the lesson or transformation that could come from them. These trials reignited my passion and led me to my vision.

One of the many challenges on my life path, one of the biggest challenges I overcame, was a battle with the life-threatening disease of leukemia. That year long trial gave me a powerful model for how to overcome any life challenge, find the light, rise back up and keep moving in the direction of my dreams.

The Value of Your Lessons Learned

This sudden diagnosis with leukemia happened 20 years ago, in 1994, when I was at the height of my seemingly very successful-looking career in the business world. Despite my outward success, I had been increasingly unhappy in this livelihood – so much so that I felt like I was dying, and eventually began to exhibit health symptoms. One weekend, while attending an out-of-town conference, I went to the emergency room where I received shocking news. I spent the next year in an isolation unit in the hospital for my treatment, rallying my spirit to reclaim life and conquer this life-threatening challenge.

Life changed so significantly for me from that moment forward. Most significantly, I was fueled and infused by the love energy that surrounded me from so many sources. I discovered that love is the most powerful energy in our universe, and love has the capacity to transform and heal.

When I came out of that trial, I was alive, thankfully, and I was just feeling lit up and fully enlivened. I had gone through some forgiveness that I needed to get to for old family wounds, which really freed up my heart. It also gave me a conviction, a commitment, and a pledge to claim and live my own true life purpose – to leave the career that I was in and to really go after my truer mission of consulting and coaching people to align their lives and livelihoods with their life purpose so that they can make their life a masterpiece.

I actually consider my dance with leukemia a blessing. That sentiment shocks some people, but it really was a gift to me.

One of the other lessons I learned is that we can't do it alone. I had community surrounding me, and that reinforced for me the value and power of team. I encourage clients to allow others to help them realize their vision. It could be a friend, family member or even a life coach.

A key piece about having a coach in your life, or a mentor or spiritual guide, is to have an outside resource help keep you focused on and moving towards that beautiful pleasure island that you are creating and you want to get to. When you're trying to traverse what looks like a seemingly huge gap, from the painful yet familiar place you're leaving, it can get pretty scary, and it's very human for all kinds of negative thoughts, doubts, and fears to come up and paralyze you.

Many of us could just stop, go back and say, "Well, I guess I'll just keep doing this." I encourage clients to keep their vision alive and to focus on the possibilities. I have a very structured, proven DreamBuilding program that gives all the tools that help people do that. It's a structure and a process, and as a certified DreamBuilder coach, I can guide you through.

Words of Wisdom and Vision

Dream building is a process. The process involves first being able to get a clear vision for what you would love without worrying or questioning how it can happen. *What would I love in my life now?*

Once you get clear about what you would love more of in your life, you need to paint a clear picture of what that looks like. Then, throughout the process, you're outlining, *"What can I do, what next steps can I keep taking that would take me one step closer to that dream?"*

If you think of the whole thing at one time, it can be overwhelming and be a showstopper. As Henry David Thoreau suggests in one of his most famous quotes, "What is one step that I can take to advance confidently in the direction of this dream?" Just take steps – even if you can't see where the next one is leading. Just walk up the next step of the staircase.

One of the biggest lessons I've learned – and this was key for me, and I don't think it's just true for me, I think it could be true for anyone, is this ... when significant parts of your essential essence are not able to be expressed in your world, you can really start to lose your soul. Your vibrational frequency starts to slow down, you feel dulled down, your light isn't shining as bright, and your dis-ease can turn into a disease like mine did.

This is your trip called life. Why be alive if you're not really living? I encourage people to claim their life, live it, and make it a masterpiece, even though that might sound lofty and idealistic. I think the more of us that are able to do that; the more we can send a ripple effect of Light out into the world.

We're joyful. We're creative. We're expansive, instead of constricted, fearful, and going through the rat race and the drill of life.

Carve out some time each day to have a meditative space for yourself. Maybe even put on some inspiring music. Let yourself relax. Relax your body, and just start to go into your imagination.

Our imagination is such a powerful mental faculty. It taps into all the possibilities. Let your imagination just go crazy envisioning and getting pictures of aspects of your life that you would love, and just keep asking yourself the question, "What would I love in my vocation, in my relationships, in my health and body, and in my financial freedom?"

When you come out of that meditative space, take some notes and write down this picture that came to you. Then, if you feel so inspired, I highly encourage you to get some materials like a poster board, magazines and art materials, and find images and words to put on your dream vision board. Put it somewhere in your space where you can look at it every day. It's really fun!

It is very powerful. That's how we manifest from the invisible to actually bringing something into material form on the earth - by writing down an idea or vision and then putting it in visual form. That's when it starts to get activated and brought alive.

The Talmud, which is a sacred, ancient, and central text of Rabbinic Judaism, says that, "Every blade of grass has its angel that bends over it and whispers, 'grow, grow.'" I've discovered that I am just like that blade of grass.

We're always reaching for the light. Blades of grass will press through cement seeking the light. We have angels that can lean over us and encourage us to keep growing. Seek out those angel sources for yourself – whether it's a coach, whether it's real angels, whether it's friends, colleagues ... we're designed to keep growing and to keep reaching for the light.

30. You Too Can Do
Susanne Whited

Although she was paralyzed in an automobile accident as a young mother, disabled is not a word you would use to describe **Susanne Whited**. Her can-do attitude propels her to take on challenges such as coaching children's soccer from a wheelchair and starting her own business after losing a job she loved.

Susanne is passionate about inspiring small business owners to pause for a moment and to fully design their dream business model. She then guides them on the journey to realize their business vision.

Based in Colorado, Susanne is a frequent guest on radio and television programs. She has been featured on podcasts and other expert interview venues and she regularly addresses groups as an inspirational speaker and marketing "How-to" strategist. Follow her adventures on Twitter @MyBusinessTwit.

My Vision

The biggest message I want to bring to people is to realize that they are better than they think they are. Sometimes our mind gets stuck on what we are not able to do. What we really need is to spend our time focusing on what we can do, and make that as important as we can.

My Voyage

I was living the ideal life. I was a young mother. I had a seven-year-old son and a six-and-a-half-month-old daughter. I traveled a lot for my job. I was having a great time, but then I made the mistake of falling asleep while I was driving.

I rolled my pickup, the roof caved in, and I broke my neck. I was paralyzed. One day I am running around doing everything that everybody else does, and the next day I am lying in a bed and I cannot even raise my arm off the bed.

I was very blessed with the knowledge that I had done so much before this happened that I never, ever felt that I got cheated out of life. I have been to all but five states in the United States. I have traveled to Mexico and I have also traveled Canada a few times. I had done so much, even though I was so young.

I focused on my children while rehabbing from my accident, because I had a young son and a baby, and that was where my efforts were needed. I did not have the time to worry about, "What am I missing?" All I could think about was, "What do I have, and how do I go forward from here?"

I remember when my son came to visit me the first time in the hospital right after my accident. He came in and I said, "Now, you realize that I am not going to walk again." He looked at me and said, "That is okay, Mom. We are going to put a ramp in so you can get in the house."

Where I live, I do not have any immediate family, but I had my husband for support and his family is from here, so his mother helped also. Much of my support came from reaching out to all my neighbors that I knew beforehand. "Here is what I need. Can you help me?" I got it; diaper changes, transportation for my kids, whatever I asked for.

One of the many benefits of doing rehab is they really, really knock one mantra into your head. "Quality of life is more important than independence." Yes, you could put on your own makeup, and it is going to take you two hours, but somebody can help you do your makeup and it takes you 15 minutes. Which is the better use of your time? I really bought into that idea of determining what is really worth me doing by myself, and what is better to let somebody else do so I have a better quality of life.

It is hard to remember to accept help from strangers; I still sometimes say "No." when people try to help me. Somebody will come by while I am going in a door and I have done all the hard work in getting the door open. I am already halfway in the door and they say, "Can I get that for you?" I am thinking, "Well, no. I have already got it!" I do try to remember to say, "Yes, go ahead," because they want to help me. People feel better when they are able to help. Even if it is the simple task of them opening the door for me without my asking and it makes them feel better, it is as if I gave them a gift today, just by me saying, "Yes, go ahead and open that door for me." I am not afraid to ask people for help when I need it. If I am in the grocery store and there is an item on the top or bottom shelf, I will stop someone and ask, "Can you reach that for me?" Nobody has ever told me "No."

I had an experience once that shows the power of giving. Several years ago, I was in the mall with my kids. A lady is walking towards me, and then she walks in front of me, so I scoot over, and then she scoots back over to block me, and then she stops me.

I do not look like a homeless person, but she gave me $40, and she says, "I love to see you out with your kids. I want to pay for your day." I took that money, and the next day I was at the doctor's office and I am talking to this man. He is telling me about how he is out of money and he is getting ready to go down to Florida to look for work. When I went into the doctor's appointment, I gave the $40 to the receptionist and said, "When that man comes out, will you give this to him, because he needs this way more than I do."

It really is a small world, because about eight months later, he had come back to our town. He was working in the park next to that doctor's office and he saw me go into the doctor's office. He came up and he said to me, "You know, I really needed that money at that time and I really appreciate what you did."

The woman that gave me the money, she never knew. It made her feel good, but I passed it on, and look at what I got out of it.

The Value of Lessons Learned

What I really try to focus on is staying positive and happy. I really am a glass half-full kind of person. I wake up in the morning, and I wake up half out of it like everybody else does, but once my brain starts working, I really do think I am going to have a great day, and I make that a point. "I am going to have a great day."

When I sign my emails, most the time I close with, "Have a great day." I write that out. It is not copied and pasted into my signature. I write it out every time to remind myself that I need to have a great day.

I do think that you have to always think full circle. If you bring positive in, you are going to get positive out. If you are always thinking negatively, that is what is going to happen. If you wake up every day and think, "Today is going to be horrible. It is Monday; I do not like Mondays!" you will have a horrible Monday. You know what? Monday is just like every other day of week. Do I have a little bit more pep in my step on Mondays than I have on Fridays? Yes, I do. By the time Friday comes around, I may be worn out. So on Monday I may have a little bit more energy than Friday, but Fridays can be just as great as a Monday, or a Wednesday can be just as great as a Saturday. It is what you put into it.

Words of Wisdom and Vision

I really love teaching people how to accomplish tasks for themselves. I think it comes back to that independence that I have. I want to be able to do as much as I can for myself, and I want other people to be able to do as much as they can for themselves, especially with social media. People get started with it and they are all confused about, "How do I do this? How do I do that?" It is really simple once somebody shows you, but you do not know what you do not know.

I started our Twitter feed at a job many years ago. They said,

"We need somebody to do it."

"Okay, I will."

It turns out, I love Twitter. It is my absolute favorite. It is short, sweet, and to the point. It tells me what you want, and maybe I will do it. That is how Twitter is. Here is a headline; here is a link. It is great for someone like me who just wants to scan through information. "That one is interesting. I will click on it and I will find out more."

When I was reading my Twitter feed, I would see accounts that would just post really random pieces of information that did not relate to their business at all. I would ask the owners, "How is that helping your business?" People said, "My social media guy told me if I go to the store, post it to my account." Nobody following you cares that you are going to the store. You have to think about your end user. You do not want to waste their time.

I try to get business owners to think about focusing their social media around their business, and not get overwhelmed. So many social media experts say, "You have tweet X times a day and post on Facebook five times a day and write a blog every single day or three times a week, or make a video every week." People keep hearing this, and it freaks them out.

I really try to explain to them that if you can write the newsletter you send out to your email list comfortably every other week, then do it every other week. If you can do a video once a month and it makes you happy doing it once a month, then do it once a month. If doing it once a week would stress you out, do not do it every week. Be very realistic when you set your time budget for your work and content schedule so that you are not feeling overwhelmed.

That is actually what I call my social media program – Stop the Social Media Madness. Do not get into this free fall of, "I have got to do this, and I have got to do that." There are tools that can simplify it for you. Use them and make it simpler than you think it is.

The biggest tip I would offer is when you get up every day, you have to decide, "This is going to be a great day. I am going to have a good day. I can be happy today, or I can be miserable."

I am very, very fortunate. I do not have any pain associated with my injury. I know people that have a lot of pain. It is really hard for them to overcome that and get that good positive attitude. Wherever you are at – and this is another of the best realizations that happened to me when I did rehab – sure, I cannot transfer myself in and out of my wheelchair and I have to use a power chair because I am not very strong, but there were people I rehabbed with on ventilators who could not breathe for themselves. Every day, every breath that I get to take on my own without a machine breathing for me, I am better off than somebody else.

There is always something you have that you can be thankful for. Look for it, embrace it and Have a Great Day!

31. Your Rites of Passage
Rev. M. Azima Jackson, MS, DMin

Rev. Mary Azima Jackson uses energetic healing, song, meditation, counseling, and ceremony for life's rites of passage. This leads to greater self-discovery and reinvention.

She is an ordained Interfaith Minister with a Doctorate in Ministry, Masters in Divinity from Yale Divinity School, and Masters in Biological Sciences. Chopra University recognizes her as Vedic Master: certified to teach Primordial Sound Meditation, Yoga, and Perfect Health. She has served as Chaplain at Yale New Haven and Griffin Hospitals.

Azima is well versed in both Eastern and Western approaches to music. She has produced two CDs, *Passages Through Light*, and *Angel Love*. Azima is Director of House of Light and co-founder of Ageless Secrets. She is co-executive producer of the documentary, *Awaken Your Riches* and co-author of the book, *The Change*. She conducts retreats Extraordinary Living-Fearless Dying. She is the Master Trainer of the GPS Code. info@age-lesssecrets.com

My Vision

It starts with oneself. From there, like a pebble in a pool with its circles, I would love to see more people "wake up" and become more aware of how great they are; to be able to look at their own light within and allow that light to be shared with other people around them.

As one person, you can't just say, "I want everything to be better," and fix the world. Each person can make the world a better place as they change themselves. They are able to respond from their wounded places. That is the place where there is a portal opening to the reality of their beauty. From there, they can shine a little more with the gifts that they have brought to this life, and others will receive from that.

I'm thinking of that game where one person touches another, then another. One circle opens up to another circle. Eventually, more people will find that light within themselves, that love, that caring, that compassion for themselves, and therefore for others. It expands into an ever-greater sort of dynamic circle of being, and that's how I think you help to heal the planet, starting with yourself.

My Voyage

I think I started like anyone else, and I wasn't even thinking or feeling a whole lot, except getting through each day. At some point, I ended up with a lot of pain. When I was in college, it was eventually diagnosed. It was called Crohn's Disease, and it's supposedly a chronic illness that can cause death. I actually nearly died a couple of times and went through very painful medical processes – so much so that I realized that it was almost more painful to go to the hospital than to find another way to heal.

That's what eventually brought me to new understandings. One was a greater awareness of complementary medicine. I began to look at energy and how energy not only affects us, which was my first understanding. I came to realize that we're actually made of energy.

Through energy, one can do a great deal of healing. For me, it was music. It was the vibration of music and songs. In my worst period of pain, I began to hear melodies that were singing through me and dissolving the pain. I later came to realize that it was angels that were passing on messages that eventually became a CD, *Angel Love*.

Another important aspect of my journey was my relationship to God. Who or what is God? My understanding of God began in a particular religion, Christian. That expanded, over time, to interfaith. I now believe that each faith comes from the same source. It is the culture that determines what that religion looks like. We all come from the same source. It depends on the language and the culture as to how we perceive this source.

My journey has shown me that energy healing, music, and interfaith celebrations of a variety of ceremonies have been pivotal to my healing. I now know that this helps me to support others more enthusiastically, because that's been my path.

The Value of Lessons Learned

Some lessons were learned more slowly than others; however, this is the way life is, I think. It's almost like the challenge was made for each person just for that person's growth. We're all unique in terms of where our challenge rests.

For me, I think my challenges began before I was even born. For most people, it's the period of time either before you're born in the uterus, or up until about the age of eight. It's almost like a hypnotic time when that little child takes on conditioning from their caretakers, from their parents, from the ones who are important to them. At the time, they're so little that these perceptions seem like very big things that are determining their life. As we get bigger and grow older, we don't realize that these are preconditioned standards that have been imprinted on us or belief systems that we've taken on, and we live from. It's almost like we don't grow up. It's as if our adult lives are ruled by our childhood patterns. It's like a continuum of those same blocks.

For me, the blocks had to reveal themselves by nearly killing me. I didn't come to think about, "Oh my gosh, there might be something else or a way I can survive." When I became repeatedly in so much pain, I started looking at my life. I started to understand that there might be something here that if it's revealed to me and as it's revealed to me, I can open up a little more to love for myself and therefore for others. This compassion was for what I didn't understand when I was a child and as I grew up. I didn't see, understand or realize, that these were all pretty concretized belief systems that I had taken on.

I think part of the journey is coming to recognize what these obstacles have been, with compassion, and realizing that we are greater than this, and can move beyond and through this. Trust is one of the most important elements that guide us through this journey. I'm still in the process of learning how to trust more, have more faith in the fact that there is something greater than my mental understanding.

Even though we are unique in our own way, the human condition has common denominators. I see the possibility for each of us is to find that inner light within us and to let it shine.

One of the things I love is officiating at wedding ceremonies and creating lasting memories. I enjoy performing weddings that are interfaith. Recently, I married a Christian woman to an Indian man. It brought out the best of both cultures and was well received. Yet another memorable wedding that comes to mind is the one held under a weeping Beech tree whose limbs and branches were expansive enough to cascade around the wedding party. The wedding honored two musicians and approximately 50 other musician friends who came to celebrate their wedding. The blessings were through music. It was truly a musical wedding that celebrated the harmony of love.

Baby blessings are especially heart warming. Often, couples I have married have called me when it is time to bless their baby.

I have also performed memorial services. It is an honoring both those who have moved on with their stories, as well as those who are still here.

The above are rituals that I enjoy performing. I have realized their importance in celebration and rites of passage. Included in this, and especially dear to my heart, is music and songs.

Songs I have written have been real communications to me. Sometimes, in the beginning, I won't even understand what is coming through me. I'll just write the words down and the music, and then I'll look back at it and say, "Oh my gosh. Thank you. What a gift."

Music, rituals that I mentioned above, and so many more, are means of becoming more conscious. I'm also delving into consciousness research with Tianna Conte and focusing on Extraordinary Living and Fearless Dying. I am training with Tianna in the GPS Code, which is a simple system for accessing innate guidance and power.

I am committed to becoming more conscious, and in so doing can be best able to empower others. It is recognizing, that as Teilhard de Chardin best expresses it, "We are not human beings having a spiritual experience. We are spiritual beings having a human experience."

Words of Wisdom and Vision

If I think of music, I'm going back to one thing that was fun that I learned from Pat Moffett Cook, and that was if you play small amounts of different varieties of music, you take someone who is with you on a music journey. They just speak aloud the journey they're going through as they listen to this music. As you play two or three different kinds of music, they go on a journey and then come back again. It's fascinating how that helps reveal some of what could be one's goal, what could be one's aspirations without them really being conscious of it. It's just slightly below the conscious knowledge, and the music helps bring out what their desires would be.

Meditation is another helpful tool in rising one's consciousness by quieting the mind. I, myself, sometimes have trouble with meditation, but there are a variety of ways of meditating. People use walking meditation. I find that music helps me put myself in a meditative mood if I listen to it or if I play it. Otherwise, I've trained with Deepak Chopra so I can do primordial sound meditation that includes a mantra. Another form of meditation is sitting silently with the object being your breath. You can do this first with your eyes closed and then your eyes open to basic awareness.

I think what's important, where I've gotten stuck and I think some people get stuck often, is that they get hooked on their storyline, whether it be a past story or something that they would want to have happen. If you call it a goal – sometimes I shrink when I think "goal." Tianna provided me with a helpful suggestion that works for her. Instead of a goal she calls it a vision. A vision is allowed to unfold in its own time without our need to make it happen. It is an interesting differentiation. Whereas a goal seems to come from our conscious logical mind, vision seems to emerge from our heart and soul.

Sometimes just the way one speaks about goals can be scary. Answers and direction can come to you when you are not so caught up in your mind. You can step into that quiet space of guidance through the music, through meditation. Some people do it through dance. I've known people that do it through movement. It doesn't have to be official dance – just moving to music, things can be revealed that you wouldn't otherwise think of.

That's the key. How would each particular person be helped to be more aware of what it is that they love doing? What are the places where they lose track of time where they really enjoy doing this or that? What is it that's calling them? There are different ways of finding those interests in each person, depending on the person.

I come from the Sufi Order International tradition. The pir, or head of the order, a few years back, used to say his goal was to have a beautiful world filled with beautiful people. My desire is to be able to, in my way, help to let other people, myself included, all grow into more of a beautiful world with more beautiful people. That means people who are responsible, people who are living fully their human life as open to their spiritual and divine inheritance as they can be at any given time. Let us awake and surrender to the fact that each of us has our own inner guidance that will lead us into being more beautiful people in a more beautiful world.

32. Sneak Peek to Possibilities
Dr. Tianna Conte, N.D.

Tianna Conte is a trail blazing blend of mystic, scientist, and best-selling transformational author. She is a trained naturopath, interfaith minister, and initiated shaman specializing in mind-body therapy. She has been empowering people in personal evolution for forty years. Integrating ancient wisdom with cutting-edge energy psychology has earned her a reputation as a "physician" to the soul.

Her Near-Death Experience uniquely qualifies her to bring a deep intuitive knowledge of consciousness, life, death and transformation to the eternal journey.

Tianna focuses on training others to live life with passion, purpose, and pleasure. She is the director of Infinite Possibilities Productions, co-founder of Ageless Secrets and co-author of *Love's Fire* trilogy and *The Change*. She is the producer whose story is featured in *Awaken Your Riches*, and co-stars in *Dying To Live*. Currently in private practice, she conducts retreats in Extraordinary Living-Fearless Dying. Through international travels, and participation with shamans and spiritual masters, Tianna has explored the evolutionary power of love-based living. The result has been the creation of the GPS Code for accessing one's innate guidance and power. http://www.age-lesssecrets.com

My Vision

I was a nine-year-old child, and I had a dream that this woman came from the stars and put something in my hands, and it glowed. I put it in the hands of somebody else, and then it glowed for them. I saw a picture of the globe of the world. The world was dark, because people had wounds in health, money, relationships, and all sorts of things. As this was put into their hands, the world turned to light.

At that time, of course, I had no idea what it was about. I remember turning to my dad, who was always my hero mentor, and he was amazing. He exclaimed, "I don't understand that dream, but it's a precious one. Keep it close to your heart, and one day your soul will let you know what that dream was about."

I never realized, with the twists and turns and everything in life, my work would go into energy medicine, writing, and speaking. The globe of light is energy, energy in the form of wisdom, contained in my best-selling books, documentary and GPS Code system that I am excited to present. It just kept evolving.

My vision is that people have more power than they realize. They have more wisdom than they realize; and when you break free from conditioned thinking, anything's possible. My passion is all about how to help people break free from conditioned living. Respect the rules, and stretch it to make it uniquely you. That's been the essence.

My Voyage

In 1995, I had a near-death experience (NDE)– not a near-death experience through accident or illness – but in a body wrap at a spa. I didn't even know it was a NDE at that time. It was the most amazing experience. It was mystical and bringing to life everything we know about who we truly are as beings beyond just physical form, beyond a brain that's just a limited mind – that we are each individual expressions of a frequency. I very affectionately call it a God frequency, love frequency – whatever anybody wants to call it.

After that, my life was never the same. I couldn't do therapy the same. I couldn't do anything the same. I remember saying to my then fiancé, "We need to recreate this experience for others." He looked at me and said, "Honey, you know I support you in all that you do, but not this time."

I persisted, "Why not this time?"

He said one word – "Liability."

I guess, yes, recreating a NDE is a little bit hazardous. However, in the course of everything and to the present day, with the books, with this amazing doctor's work in quantum physics of shifting consciousness at a core level, and my GPS Code, I am excited that we have the closest access to a NDE without the liability.

The GPS Code is hot off the presses, it's not even in print yet – I received a vision of a new system that is my legacy to pass on of my individual work. For those who are comfortable with the word God, "God-Source Positioning System," and it's the code I believe we all hold in our DNA to awaken our innate ability to navigate guidance for our lives. There's even an energy machine that's NASA-based that raises people's frequency.

My voyage actually started very, very young, because my dad was, as I said, my hero mentor. He was a medical doctor in the 1950s, and he was beyond a medical doctor. Without calling it a 'healer' back then, he always connected life and what was going on with his patients.

I have the gift of clairvoyance. I didn't know that everybody didn't have that gift. To me, I could look at the body and see where the issues were. I would go down to his office as a precocious little girl. Those were the days you didn't have appointments, you come with your lunch, your knitting, you just sat in the office around a circle until you were called by the doctor. I would see these people go in. They were energetically dark. I would put my hand on them to help bring more light.

I would say, "Can I put hands on boo-boo and make it better?" I would do this. They'd go in and they'd come out, and they were filled with light. They were a transformed person. I got to see this at a very young age. I always encourage parents to listen to what your children tell you rather than what you want them to be when they grow up. Have them tell you what they want to be by what they do easily.

One day my dad had a patient he could not diagnose. I kept looking at the man and seeing a face of a mosquito. A mosquito! I proclaimed, "Daddy, I don't know if this could help, but I think I have the answer for you."

He looked at me like, "Okay, sweetheart, what can you tell Daddy that this man has?"

I said, "I see the face of a mosquito."

He ran out like when you see somebody get that 'ah-ha' moment where they just light up like a Christmas tree. He went to his medical books. He came back and inquired, "How did you know that?"

I said, "I just saw that."

He mentioned, "But how did you know that?"

I repeated, "I just saw that. It's a mosquito."

It was malaria. He had never seen a case of malaria in New York in the 1950s. That's what started it. He invited me inside the sacred halls of his practice. I would watch how whatever symptom somebody had, he'd put his hands on that area. Let's say they had an issue with their heart. "What's going on in your life that's breaking your heart?" These were not today's new age people. This is a 1950s Italian practice where they'd say, "Oh doctor, my husband is giving me ..." My father would say, "That's anger" or "That's pain" or "That's sadness. You've got to look at that. You've got to talk to your husband. You've got to make peace with that. You can't let that get to your body. It's hurting you." I watched mind/body medicine from infancy, practically.

At age nine, they all said, "You're going to be a doctor like your Daddy." What child knows this in that time? I was clear, "I want to be a doctor, but not like my Daddy. Not with drugs and surgery. I'm going to teach people about energy and how they can make themselves better."

Everybody laughed and teased, "That's such a cute little girl."

I did the traditional premed, go to med school, that kind of thing. Then, I had a tragedy that I'd rather not get into right now, but it took me way off that journey except enough to say that there are no accidents, coincidences, or mistakes. Now quantum physics proves that to be true. We're all guided, always, whether we can see it or not, because I never, ever, ever thought I'd go back into the healing arts.

I was shattered. My first fiancé was killed in a car accident, and I had a miscarriage – that's what happened. I couldn't stay with my studies. I left, and one day I get a knock at my door and it's a man from Haiti. He was selling cookware. Who would think that a vendor selling cookware would transform my life? We never know in what form a master or your next angel is going to come.

He came in, and he told us about El Salvador and what they were doing, and Haiti, and what they were doing. I started traveling. I traveled the world. Each place I went, they took me to their voodoo people, their shamans, and their medicine men. It's like the indigenous people knew that I was to be working with altered states of consciousness. I traveled the world studying altered states of consciousness.

Even though I was learning all this stuff, I never thought I'd go back to anything related to transformation through body/mind. What ended up happening was one day I was supposed to meet a client in New York, and there was the first, I think, conference on body/mind medicine. My client never showed up. I was a little pissed off. I huffed, "Okay, I'm just going to sneak into this conference."

There it went. I realized what I had seen as a child. I realized what I had learned from all the different travels I'd been doing around the world with the native shamans, and I started studying quite consciously mind/body medicine with degrees in Gestalt synergy with Ilana Rubenfeld. I worked with Jean Houston and other pioneers. I had my practice and working with people before I had all the degrees that I subsequently evolved.

I make a joke that my life is "ass backwards" – I do things before and then get the mortal thing afterwards. The mystical comes first and the mortal follows. I even did that with my marriage. I had the honeymoon first and then the marriage followed. It was a series of total guidance from beyond the beyond.

Ultimately, the GPS Code itself came from the mystical part of me because of the clairvoyance, and later I found out clairsentience and clairaudient and clair-everything else that I had. I was guided.

We're all guided. That's the key thing. We are all guided. The only difference with me because of the parallel senses to the physical senses is I get a sneak peek. I used to call myself a sneak peek to the possibilities and potentials that we all have. That's how I worked my practice. People used to say, "What do you call yourself?"

"I don't know." I didn't know what to call myself. It was nothing clear. This is way before people called themselves coaches. The closest thing was I heard Jean Houston once say "thera-pea-ist" was the therapy of the Gods. I used to say, "Okay, I'm a thera-pea-ist, not a therapist." People would say, "You just have to have an experience." That's how my personal work and transformation and helping people transform whatever issues they wanted to have came about.

My vision for my own life was I wanted to have things I could pass on and put in people's hands. I want the power in people's hands. Wouldn't you know, best-selling author of three books, a movie based on *Think and Grow Rich,* of which I co-star with Michael Beckwith, T. Harv Eker, Mark Victor Hansen- my own mentors. None of this was through clear knowing.

I'm the antithesis of the person who says you have to know your dream. No. If your dream comes to you, mazel tov – then you know your dream. To even those who say, "I don't know my dream," know that you have a dream and you are the gift. Everyone was born with a gift inside them. Here's the default message I have that I used to tell my clients was the secrets and shortcuts. You could know if you know, and then you could be clear and you could be one of those people who know their goals, or you could be like me. You default to a power greater than you that you truly are the essence and expression of and say, "You know, you made me, you know it all – do it through me!" Viola! You will have an extraordinary life without even knowing how you got there.

The Value of Lessons Learned

Now with the GPS Code, the first words I heard that launched my journey were when my incredible mentor/hero father died – a very sacred wound happened on that day to me that could either destroy a person or awaken a power. I was blessed with having that power awakened through a sexual violation and death on the same day. I've got tears in my eyes because I never thought I'd be sharing that with the world, and guidance says it's time to show people your transparent truth. "Yes, you've got all these mystical gifts and all these great things, but look at the wound and go there and share that."

The words I heard, which have been the cornerstone of my life and now the cornerstone of this code are, "Surrender each day, step by step. You'll be shown the way." Every day I would talk to this invisible power like I used to talk to my Dad. "Good morning God, or whoever you are or whatever you are. This is who I am. This is how I am today. What do you want of me and how are you going to use me?"

When I was in pain and screeching after all that had happened, we were blessed enough to live on the water and I heard those words. I was also filled with a mystical light. Spielberg could not have scripted it better. It was a cloudy day. The clouds parted. The sun came out. This beam of light filled me from top to toe, every cell, with love, and I heard those words. That was my waking up, transformative, spiritual moment that became the guiding light of my life through the darkness.

That's what I want to pass on to people, that there's a force greater than us, that is us, through us that can transform anything. The key is, never give up and never give in. The one time I almost did try to give in was when my fiancé passed and the miscarriage that I talked about – and I never thought I'd share this with living souls. However, with what's happened on the planet today and especially with the beauty of the force of Robin Williams, I knew I needed to open the conversation on suicidal thoughts.

I had had enough. I was in my twenties. I was going to take a bottle of vodka and sleeping pills and end it all. I couldn't open the childproof cap on the sleeping pills. In those days before my training of understanding, if I drank the whole bottle of vodka that would have done it. I went to get a hammer to break the bottle. This energetic force held my hand back, and I heard the words again. "Surrender each day, step by step. You'll be shown the way."

At that point, I knew. I had heard stereo. I would never, ever do that again, because who was I to take away my life when there were so many people who were hurting more and I'd been given so many gifts to pass on?

I was at our land in Costa Rica, and a little insect bit me. I didn't think anything of it, until I found out after everything healed, that it was a cousin of the brown recluse spider. I had this poisonous venom that had to be pulled out. The GPS Code was born from looking at the hole in my toes that was created by this poisonous spider. I saw five gears and five hand signals. Now I can actually take all of my years of training and give people a system that is deceptively simple to follow.

I've got all these things that that little girl wanted to put in people's hands. Books, and now this book that I'm honored to be part of ... *The Voyage To Your Vision*. Yes, people, whether you know your vision, whether you don't know your vision, your vision knows you. All you have to do is take a step at a time in the direction that your heart and your intuition move you. It will take you to a journey and into possibilities and into greatness the limited conscious mind just cannot go.

We're not designed for that, and quantum physics now tells us we are these incredible beings of energy and light with all potential. Here's the beautiful part – it doesn't require a lot of heavy training. It goes across genders, across cultures, across sexes, across religions, across everything. At our core, we are all connected. We are pieces of a puzzle to a grander super puzzle.

As much as that part of my work has been because of my own wounds, the mystery school approach to working with me or hearing from me the Universe had other plans. So now I am to be more visible through books, movies, and the GPS Code. The wisdom that comes from just picking up a book of inspiration of, "If others can do it, I can do it, you can do it, we can all do it, and we can all pass it on." We all have the potential to pass it on. It's a new form of enlightenment, I would say, for lack of a better word.

That's the version of my journey, and then as I mentioned, my incredible second fiancé then became my husband. That's a whole other controversial, delicious story because of my gifts. When he passed on, and he passed on while we were in the middle of a kiss, I was giving him CPR. I believed he was having a NDE, and I was calling him back to me. Instead, I went with him into the Light and then he continued on and I was sent back.

I hate to confess it, and it's true. Am I going to be the one that writes the book, *Rejected By The Light*? When people have rejection issues I used to have them crack up laughing because I would say, "If you think you have fear of rejection for your success, imagine being rejected by the Light. That's the ultimate rejection. If I can laugh at that, you can laugh at rejection from a source who probably doesn't know your greatness or who you are. Do not give up. Do not give in. Keep on taking a step at a time. Surrender each day, and step by step you'll be shown the way."

That became my little joke. When people say, "I can't do success because of the fear of rejection." "Well, I was rejected by the Light, and I'm still ticking." Again, because of my gifts, I started hearing and feeling my departed husband and thinking, "I'm a doctor now – post-traumatic stress disorder." Then the mediums, the mystics, the spiritual teachers who know me said, "No, no, no. You have the gift." Even Raymond Moody called me a living bridge of possibilities between the worlds.

All the training that you see that I've had with the shamans in the altered states and the gifts I was born with, all came to play and now my ultimate message to people is love and life never dies. It does transform. So really live your life to the fullest, dream to the highest; let the people you know know you love them. Keep your priorities really, really strong, because when death happens, that loss is real and the emotions and the grieving is very painful.

Life never dies. That's why the beauty of the mediums who talk about hearing and feeling, you will be reunited. I'm living a strange life. When I took my marriage vows and to forever say, "Happily ever after" I never realized it would be "Happily from the hereafter." It's wild. I could not have scripted my life consciously. I daresay if you can, mazel tov, do it – but even if you can't, my message is there's a force that breaths us, that beats our hearts, that is one with all of us, that has a bigger dream for you than you could ever dream. Just get out of your own way and let that force drive.

William, my beloved, before he passed away, one day he was totally bedridden, laughing and laughing. He announced, "I finally found the ultimate secret I've been seeking and the cosmic joke of the Universe."

I exclaimed, "Oh please tell me! Please, please!" Who doesn't want that?

He responded, "Picture a stretch limousine and you think you're the driver. You're really in the back seat. Put your feet up and let the driver drive."

Even with all of my mystical trainings and altered state, I laughed as though I knew it, but I didn't have a clue.

It has taken me decades to get it. As the Universe would have it, after he passed away and I went on a grieving journey of all proportions, I ended up in Costa Rica with a spiritual master. He said – and this is to people now of Law of Attraction – (I was teaching "You Create Your Reality" back in the 1980s. I was one of the prime teachers of that one.) He said, "There's no such thing as free will."

I was like, "What?"

Then he said, "Picture a stretch limousine and you think you're the driver."

I almost fainted and my nails almost clawed into his designer furniture. He changed it just a little bit. He continued, "You're in the back seat with a baby plastic steering wheel in front of you, and you get to play with that steering wheel. When that steering wheel turns left and you go left, you think you created that. The car was going to turn left anyhow."

I went, "Oh my God – I'm starting to get the picture."

However, I still didn't get the full picture until one day I was driving my own car, and my little Shih Tzu who had just gotten groomed was whining. I opened up the case so he could pop his little head out, but of course, leave it to Starsky, he didn't just pop his head out. He popped his whole body out. It was like a birthing out of this little tiny hole I had created, and he was on my lap and he had his paws on the steering wheel, and he was driving my car like he was driving. He was having the time of his life moving the wheel.

I realized, "I'm really driving the car." Then William, laughingly from beyond, because I could hear and feel him at times, declared, "Gotcha!" and that picture came to life. Oh my goodness.

Words of Wisdom and Vision

With our conscious mind, with our ego personality self, we do our best to steer and guide the voyage of our lives. However, our higher nature, the God self, the beings that we all are, that's really guiding our journey and driving our lives. Sometimes, we're attuned enough to hear those dreams and see those visions, and other times we are driving blindly. If we trust that there's a light and a power greater than us coming through us and learn to still the chatter of the monkey mind and open up to the stillness of the wisdom of who we truly are, then that voyage can be one that is amazing.

Everyone deserves it. Everyone's story is unique and everyone's gifts are unique. I daresay, we all have gifts and our own uniqueness, and we're all here to make individual, community, and global differences. I'm honored to be in this book with

Marcia Wieder, with Rick Frishman who I know, and all in making that wave, that ripple that has endless possibilities of awakening at a time that the greatest shift is taking place on the earth right now. Everyone, in their own way, is waking up to we are bigger than what we appear to be.

Our bodies are infinite and have abilities to heal themselves, transform themselves, all sorts of stuff. Our minds are not limited by beliefs that we made up from wounds from our childhood. When we let that go, we are infinite beings with infinite possibilities. That's my journey. Let it speak to the destiny that is yours.

33. HOPE
Carol Davies

Carol Davies, the Passion Motivator, is a success coach, writer and inspirational speaker based in Canada. She has an international practice that supports her many clients to discover and follow their true passions. She guides her clients to be the best they can be, finds out in what areas they may be blocked, clears these blockages and then makes a solid life plan with achievable goals to follow their true passions.

Carol's mission is to awaken people to their real life passion and life purpose through her unique HOPE (Have Optimal Personal Excellence) program, the best job she's ever had as a coach, where her natural talents let her be of service to other people. Carol is also a published author of numerous books including being a contributing author to *The Gratitude Book* projects and the recent best sellers *Ready, Aim, Captivate!* and *Ready, Aim, Inspire*! www.thepassionmotivator.com

My Vision

My vision is to be a guide and a mentor for people who are looking to live authentic, abundant, purposeful, and joyful lives.

My Voyage

I have quite a diverse background working with multicultural people over a period of years. I worked for a long time with the United Nations in New York and Geneva doing information management and also learning how to be a manager and coach for people in our organization. I found I had a real gift for working with people to help them find out what they really wanted to do in their careers, and often mixed with problems in their personal life. I would be the person people came to in the organization unofficially, so I helped a lot of people over time.

Then I thought when I was ready to go into the private sector again, "What would I like to do the most?" That was to be a success coach, to help people find as much joy and satisfaction as I've been able to find in life over studying many years and finding out a lot of what I needed to do, and help people find that way to live their life more easily and joyfully, too. I have as I said quite a lot of experience with people in many different cultures. I just try to be as authentic as I can to be there to help them find their way as well.

The Value of Lessons Learned

A lot of the challenges that I met in life were having feelings of never totally being worthy of love, recognition, or financial success. I projected a strong, confident outer mask, but inside I felt like a very scared, small child looking for validation from outside sources. I put on this really wonderful persona that all was well in my world, but inside a lot of the times I was just lost and afraid.

It took me a long time overcoming different personal challenges to understand and embrace the belief that everything I need to be a success comes from within me. I feel that part of this is because I grew up in a world where there was the thought that we aren't really good enough for anything, and feelings of low self-esteem.

We all know that our lives are full of challenges and triumphs. We say, "I can't do this. I will never overcome that." It's the inner beliefs we have in ourselves that guides our journey. I decided that as a coach, I look at myself as a life design expert for others in need of help and guidance to find their life vision and their life purpose. If we're clear about what our mission is here on earth, then we can concentrate on what is most important in life. I overcame a number of personal, emotional, and spiritual challenges just through doing a lot of work, and finally just believing in me.

I found that many of the ideas I kept coming back to were having hope in myself, for others and for the future, because if I am the best that I can be and I know what is important for myself and how to live my life with the core values that lead me forward, then that will make me the best person I can be, and then I become a beacon to other people to show them also how to live their life in the best way.

It's a personalized program, because what is best for me is not necessarily the best way for someone else to live their life authentically, because they have different experiences, hopes, and dreams that are different from mine. Each person has a different life path. If they can find the tools to help them clarify what's most important and what they wish to give to the world, that is how they too become a beacon to lead other people.

My biggest life lesson is that everything I need is within me. I don't need to be validated by other people or other beliefs. It's the belief in me, that, as I uncover what is important for me that I have the strength and the passion to be able to bring these gifts out. As I do that, I just get more and more empowered. That is empowering for other people because I then become a guide and an example; a beacon.

For me, my legacy would start at the personal level, and then as one becomes clear about the message they have and then they share that with other people, one by one it will spread and affect others to also share similar values and to live life as positively as possible.

What I see is a global legacy of positivity and belief that everything in the world that we need is there for our use, and to make a difference by taking all the tools and the gifts that life has given us and giving them to other people who will then learn from those and go on to reach others. It's really like a ripple effect.

Words of Wisdom and Vision

When I'm working with people to help them clarify their goals and move forward in life, I crystallized it down to six different steps. The first one that's very important is ***always keep learning new things***. I constantly ask my clients to check with themselves with new knowledge that they have. Will it be useful for them for helping themselves and pursuing their own dreams? Find a way to implement that knowledge and test the doubt.

The second one is ***learn from your mistakes***. Don't stay stuck in the past. I say to myself and have my clients say, "I made a choice that maybe didn't work out the way I wanted, so now I choose to make another choice and go forward." It's as simple as that. Stay in the present.

The third step is ***learn who you are***. Know your strengths, passions, weaknesses, talents, gifts, values, successes and failures. I ask people to dig inside themselves and test out their thoughts. When you discover what you're really good at and your strengths and concentrate on those, that's when you go forward.

The fourth step, I also ask people to **write down their experiences**. For example, journaling daily about what's happening, what they're learning, what they love, what they don't like, what they're good at, and what inspires them, because every emotion and lesson, positive and negative that's written down and looked back over, it forms your story and how you can use it to better learn from whatever happened before and go forward. Always go forward.

Then, when you're learning things and things are becoming clear, teach these things to other people. There's no better indication of true knowledge than when you can genuinely help and teach someone else what you've learned. I always ask people to give of themselves. We're here to learn to serve and help others.

I would say the last step is to ***be true to yourself***. Be authentic. That is most important.

Words of Wisdom and Vision

ALCHEMY OF TRANSFORMATION

"Vision is a projection of imagination. Imagination is 'Images-in-action' - Motion Pictures - Hollywood.

All manifestation starts in the imagination (cause) and transforms into reality (effect).

Whatever moving pictures are constantly running on the screen of your mind, are projecting onto the scenario of your life and driving it, whether you want it or not.

In your imagination, you are the scriptwriter, the director and the central actor of your life; this is where you get to rehearse the events of your life, past or future.

Higher dimensions of realty are also accessed through this process."

By Nano Daemon
http://www.nanodaemon.com

Rediscover and Follow Your Dreams

"Rediscover and follow your dreams is one of the most important things I can say. Our vibration and emotional energy is what guides us to a fulfilling and happy life. Unfortunately most of us are stuck in negative low energy and a low emotional vibration, which brings with it more unhappiness and feelings of unfulfillment.

By just starting to move in the direction of your dreams, you can change your vibration and emotional energy. When your vibration and energy are up, that is when the magic happens in a person's life. This creates the shift that changes your life of struggle to a life of your dreams."

By Adriana Ellis
Better Life Coach
Attuned Wholistic Services
www.attunedws.com

Heal Your Heart and Free Your Mind!

The voyage to your vision is one of the most important journeys you will ever go on! It is a voyage into your heart and deep into to your subconscious mind that leads you to awakening your heart, and unblocking all of its power! It will make clear why all of the things that have happened in your life have unfolded as they have, and lead you to living your life's purpose and your soul's true intention!

Do you know how powerful your heart is? Do you know that it is 5,000 times more powerful electromagnetically than the brain, and that it is really running the show? So how is your heart feeling right now? Is it filled with love and peace? Clear of fear, hurt or worry? How is your life right now? Would you like a few things to be different? Let me help your potent heart create an even better life experience for you now!

By Brandy Faith Weld
Author/Creator
Heal Your Heart ~ Free Your Mind book and workshop
www.HealYourHeartFreeYourMind.com
www.HealYourHeartFreeYourMindBook.com

Everyone Deserves to Be Heard™

We all want to feel fulfilled in our jobs and that often comes with a sense of being heard. Having worked in the marketing department of financial services companies for seventeen years, I often felt creatively stifled by the strict regulations regarding what you *cannot* say in the marketing materials I was responsible for producing. Not having an opportunity to flex my creative muscle caused me to suppress my voice and shut down the idea factory going on in my head, in order to be safe and go with the flow. 'Don't make waves,' my left brain said to my right brain.

We all long to be heard, understood and accepted. We seek validation that we have made a difference by being in this world. Fortunately for me, this universal need to be heard was met head on by an opportunity to assert my creativity by starting my own business in 2005 as a copywriter, where I know I *am* making a difference. I have an impact when I help my clients, who are primarily coaches, authors and speakers – which in turn allows them to help more people achieve their dreams! The ripple effect of my work in the world feels really good. Do that thing you would do even if you weren't paid to do it and make sure your voice is heard – loud and clear!

By Beverly Bergman
www.CopyForAuthors.com

Do You Need Balance?

While working one Saturday, up pops a message from my son with a link. The link goes to an ad for a sailboat. Eventually, I discovered that my son, who saw what I was ignoring regarding work-life balance, tricked me into a hobby I would love. After all, I created the business to control my destiny, not just have a job.

It is tempting to tolerate "temporary" imbalance in order to achieve the business success and financial independence. The problem starts when "temporary" drifts towards "long term," or even permanent. It happened to me. You need to step back and get control of your business, and your schedule, rather than having your business, and your customers, control you. Work ON your business, not IN your business, to transform it from what you have now to what you want. Work-life balance must be one of your business goals.

Sailing gave me critical thinking time to work ON the business, which helped it to grow. It also improved my family life. My passion is to help small business owners understand these important principles.

By Gerry Wilson
Entrepreneur & Business Coach
www.OpportunitiesBusinessAcademy.com

Your Key To Unleashing Massive Success!

Do you have an "idealized" version of yourself?
Who you think you should be?
Does the REAL you live up to the "ideal" you?
Do you criticize yourself for not "being" the ideal version...that family, society, teachers, religion have shaped?

How does that make you feel?
Empowered? Inferior?

YOU are Divine Energy individualized. The Power of "All That Is" is you. Do you believe it....know it?

The greatest successes live their lives as the fullest expression of that Power. Your deepest, juiciest joy comes from it, fueling massive success in both business and life. Allow it. Feel it. Be it.

By Deberah Bringelson
Empowerment Expert
"Bridging the Gap Between Everyday Existence and Extraordinary Results"
www.MakeYourPassionHappen.com

We Are All Storytellers

A Zen master once wrote, "*While pain is necessary, suffering is optional.*" I pondered that long and hard—in terms of how it applied both to my students and to me. The answer was surprising: we suffer when we don't know what we want to do or say. One way to avoid suffering is to write about a problem you're having.

1. Identify the issue or problem you want to work on. Then, close your eyes; try to remember the first time you became aware of the situation. The memory of this first experience will provide a greater understanding of yourself by helping you to connect your present with your past.

2. Now that you have selected the problem you want to work on and recalled a related experience, set a timer for 15 minutes. Write down what you remember about that event, and how you feel about it now.

3. Reread what you wrote and apply the five *W*'s we learned in school: Who, what, where, when, and why. Then using what you have just learned, analyze what the memory was about and how it has affected you.

4. Finally, based on the new connections you have just made between the past and the present, consider what, if any, changes you would want to make to the current situation you are writing about.

If everyone were taught to make stories out of moments in their lives as a problem-solving tool, they could easily take stock of the present, plan for the future, and/or solve an immediate problem.

By Professor Marilyn Horowitz
http://www.marilynhorowitz.com

Setbacks Can Be Setups

How many times in life do you set your goals, do the research, head in that direction so certain you're on track, but something unexpected occurs? On your way to making a difference in life, you can sometimes get derailed. In those times, do you give up on your goal or do you adjust your compass to move forward?

I had my sights set on being a full-time motivational speaker. While touring my first book, I had a life interruption called stage 3 breast cancer. Being self-employed and unable to work for nearly a year, I almost thought my dream was lost. Then I realized setbacks can be setups. I wrote another book, took on a new role as a patient advocate and developed new expertise to bring to my audiences.

Sometimes we need a particular life experience to make us more effective, compassionate or even humble. Everyone has setbacks! Steve Jobs, founder of Apple, was fired from his own company. During his "time off," he reinvented himself and came back even stronger with the iPod, iPhone, and iPad.

Don't be surprised if a setback turns into the greatest gift of your life!

By Carolyn Gross
Speaker, Author, Health Advocate
www.creativelifesolutions.com

Vision for Leadership

A good leader should be a mentor, and I've always tried to be that. I had mentors who helped me through my early years, giving me the experience necessary to proceed. I try to share that with the team members with whom I work. Bounce innovative ideas off of them, see what their reaction is, and then listen to what they're saying. Once you've done that, review it and give them some constructive guidance based on your experience. You need to ask, "Will this actually work? Is it a better solution than what we have now?"

Of course, if their ideas are good ones and result in more efficient productivity, then give them credit where credit is due. Praise never hurts. I always respect the team members' ideas and their competence. I listen to what they have to say.

Conversely, I share my experience. There is a mutual respect built up. No one knows it all, no matter how much experience or how many decades you've been at it. There are things you're not going to know that they may know. It's important to be open-minded and to have that real fluid interchange with your team members.

By Terry Zweifel
Aerospace Design Innovator
www.terryzweifel.com

The Voyage to Your Vision

Our life is a story that you are writing as you live it. Proof is all the biographies and auto-biographies in the library; each one tells a story about a person's life. The stories of voyages and travel to succeed to their own vision; the stories are different and so are the endings. Each person has a vision, a goal to succeed, a goal to maybe be famous, rich or charitable. For some, the voyage may be easy. For others, it maybe a voyage of struggle; however the goals are all the same, claim the prize.

The advantage you have is you are special, awesome and unique. You may have talents you haven't found you have yet. You have the ability to reach your visions. You need to set your vision high. You may need help on the voyage to reach your vision. You may stumble or "Fail Forward Fast." Each stumble is a lesson in what didn't work. You need to keep trying until you find what does work. It took Thomas Edison ten thousand tries to find the formula for the light bulb. You only fail when you stop trying. Good Luck!

By Jan Michael Gaynor
Jan_Gaynor@Live.com

Complimentary Resources

_____Complimentary Resources_____

Allen Klein: The Mid-Month Mirth Memo is a short amusing tidbit to brighten middle of the month monotony. It is FREE and brought to you by best-selling author, award-winning speaker, "Jollytologist"® Allen Klein. Sign up here: http://eepurl.com/t2y5T

Anne Redelfs: Are you listening to your call to awaken? Consult Anne for a free listening session to find out at annethelistener@yahoo.com OR read *The Awakening Storm* at http://theawakeningstorm.vpweb.com

Barbara Bamba: When You Don't Know Where to Start Marketing or When You'll "Ever" Have Time – Because You're Too Busy Being Stuck Behind Your Computer Learning How-To – Join Barbara's 3-Day Weekly: Make Time For Marketing: Business Development Time Block and Start Your Work-From-Home Marketing Days 5% Smarter. www.LearnBeforeULaunch.com

Carol Davies: I am so enthusiastic about helping you to attain your vision, I wish to offer you my inspiring FREE eBook, **Reach Your Full Potential**, which is filled with great tips and a plan to help you find and clarify your mission and life purpose. Go to my website www.thepassionmotivator.com and download the eBook from the homepage.

Chaffee-Thanh Nguyen: Ready to take your business to the next level and beyond? Then simply follow my 4 Step Formula For Massive Success! These four simple, yet powerful steps will ensure that you succeed in business and in life. Simply download my formula, quickly read through the short report, then start applying the concepts and watch the results! Get the report today at: www.KeyConceptCoaching.com/recommends/4stepformula/

Denise Joy Thompson: My gift to those of you who are affected by loss or trauma is a 20-minute "exploratory coaching session" to see how the loss or trauma is impacting your life. Please contact me at denise@crisisresponseconsulting.com for a complimentary discussion of how moving forward from the past can enrich your future.

Divya Parekh: What is the first step in achieving peak performance, success and breakthroughs? – Understanding yourself. You are invited to receive a Special Report Reaching Your Target: http://www.divyaparekh.com/ and Hidden Motivators Profile http://dpgroup.abeo.us/voyage (Invite Code: 44voyage) because understanding yourself will help you maximize performance by aligning opportunities with your natural motivation.

Donald Gilbert: From Dr. Don Gilbert: If you would like a free personal coaching session by phone, go to www.newlife-counseling.com and register.

Dorothy Kuhn: The WHY Business Assessment will give you instant visibility into the strength of your organization's cause, the current state of your culture, the acceptance and understanding of your cause and culture within your existing team members, and the awareness and visibility of your cause within your customer base. It is purposely set up on a sliding scale to give you the ability to assess your organization in these four key areas within the context of each other to provide you with a better perspective of your strengths and potential opportunities for improvement. To get your free WHY Business Assessment, email me at admin@powermydreams.com with subject line: "WHY Business Assessment."

Drew Hunthausen: Get a copy of Drew's free guide, *5 Keys to Living A No Excuses Life Filled With Joy, Peace, and Prosperity*. Go here to get this valuable resource: www.DrewsInspirations.com

Gary Barnes: Would you like to receive a higher return on your investment of time, energy and money? I would like to gift you my On Purpose Results Action Guide (a $97 value) for free! Go to www.garybarnesinternational.com/on-purpose-results-action-guide/ and download your personal copy today.

Geri Portnoy: Are you ready to awaken to greater freedom and deeper authenticity in your life? Discover the "Five Keys to Accelerate Your Awakening." Register at Yoga of Awakening: http://yogaofawakening.com

Hal Price: Sign-up the Heroic Heart Newsletter and also receive a free download of Hal's First eBook at http://heroicheart.org/blog/

Lauren Perotti: Would you like some tangible practices you can implement immediately for building your dream life and livelihood? Register at www.LaurenPerotti.com to claim your complimentary copy of my eBook, ***Light Your Soul-Centered Path: 7 Powerful Pillars for Living Your Divine Destiny*** now!

Rev. M. Azima Jackson: Enjoy the use of quantum tools of subtle energy technology to release stress, raise your frequency and energize your intentions. All you need is your picture and a dream. For complimentary experience, go to the membership tab at http://www.age-lesssecrets.com

Dr. Mamiko Odegard: Offers you gifts valuing over $500:
- Sample of her book, *Daily Affirmations for Love;*
- Audio from her Manthology 101 Course: "What Men Really Want You to Know" and
- A Complimentary Discovery Consultation to jumpstart you to the love and life you deserve.

Receive your bonus gifts and qualify for your Complimentary Discovery Session. ACT on Love now to start your blueprint to an EXTRAordinary YOU and your ultimate success in love and business! http://bizlifesuccessinc.com/your-voyage-to-your-vision-bonus/

Mike Fritz: Sign up at www.mikefritz.net and receive tips from Mike's eBook "#Event Love" and discover how to get people to attend and love your campus event! If you are interested in having Mike speak to your group, go to www.mikefritz.net and visit the "book Mike" page. Mike specializes in Leadership, Peak Performance and Philanthropy. Mike accepts a limited number of speaking engagements each year but would love to be a part of your event.

Paul Lawrence Vann: Excellent leadership skills is one of the most important attributes of successful people. One should possess exceptional leadership as individuals or in business and industry. Would you like to receive a motivational action eCourse to enhance your leadership abilities? Wealth Building Academy, LLC, provides a seven (7) day motivational action eCourse that provides you with the tools to increase your leadership skills and position you for more success. Register at

Live on Higher Ground:
http://liveonhigherground.com/student-ecourse/

Dr. Richard Eley: Get your free eBook: *Visioning and Goal Setting: Setting Goals to Realize the Life You Imagine.* This resource will help you focus and develop your vision, assist you in setting your goals and allow you to move towards my 5 Essential Steps to TOTAL TRANSFORMATION course. www.richardeley.com

Dr. Simone Ravicz: How well do you really know yourself? Because of the nature of our brains, egos and subconscious, there is generally quite a bit that we do not know about ourselves. Here is an excellent way to learn more and gain more clarity. Just go to the Free Personalized Assessment "Who Am I" at this link: http://successbraincoach.com/test-how-well-you-know-yourself/

From Susanne Whited: Do you find yourself reacting and acting in urgency because you do not have time to do tasks until the eleventh hour? Get a grip on your time so you can get back your life. Get your free Master Your Time guide: http://mybusinesstweets.weebly.com/free-gift.html

Dr. Tianna Conte, ND: Enjoy the use of quantum tools of subtle energy technology to release stress, raise your frequency and energize your intentions. All you need is your picture and a dream. For complimentary experience, go to the membership tab at www.age-lesssecrets.com

Viki Winterton: Write Away, Write Now! Whether you write for your own enjoyment, need marketing copy for your products and services, are an experienced author, publisher, or speaker, or are just beginning the idea stage of your book, you'll find what you need here! Receive FREE access to our global writers' community and 6-week Journaling Program! Visit: www.writeawaywritenow.com

Expert Insights Publishing: Are you a bestseller author? Want to meet some of the top writers of our time? Bestselling Authors International™ is dedicated to honoring authors across the globe who have achieved the coveted "Bestseller" status for their work. Visit free, nominate yourself or a best-selling friend for induction and enjoy your time in the wonderful world of the written word!

http://bestsellingauthorsinternational.org/

Index

Authentic/Authenticity
23, 50, 51, 52, 56, 67, 93, 140, 143, 176, 182, 195, 222, 235, 313, 316, 332

Balance
6, 20, 53, 81, 82, 87, 134, 142, 172, 189, 194, 322

Communicate/ Communication
68, 71, 92, 93, 113, 114, 142, 153, 190, 191, 198, 239, 240, 241, 261, 292

Create/Creativity
13, 17, 23, 38, 46, 55, 58, 59, 65, 90, 91, 117, 118, 122, 123, 126, 127, 128, 133, 138, 139, 140, 141, 142, 150, 152, 154, 174, 175, 178, 179, 182, 192, 193, 194, 195, 215, 229, 231, 235, 249, 253, 261, 263, 264, 272, 305, 308, 309, 319, 320, 322

Dreaming/Dreams
10, 11, 12, 13, 14, 15, 16, 17, 50, 66, 77, 79, 110, 111, 120, 151, 152, 172, 173, 182, 187, 212, 254, 274, 309, 314, 316, 319, 321, 332

Empower/Empowerment
62, 71, 72, 103, 105, 126, 139, 187, 193, 215, 257, 293, 296, 315, 323

Fulfill/Fulfillment
6, 13, 54, 104, 105, 152, 153, 162, 163, 177, 188, 209, 213, 225, 245, 319, 321

Health/Health Care
16, 31, 53, 55, 67, 68, 74, 76, 98, 113, 137, 142, 144, 191, 194, 206, 207, 208, 209, 211, 213, 225, 233, 234, 240, 256, 258, 259, 261, 274, 277, 288, 297, 325

Inspire/Inspiration/ Inspiring
15, 19, 24, 36, 38, 50, 69, 70, 90, 102, 103, 105, 112, 113, 117, 130, 132, 134, 135, 140, 143, 149, 153, 157, 159, 161, 166, 177, 182, 184, 186, 198, 204, 253, 254, 257, 259, 268, 270, 272, 277, 280, 306, 312, 316, 330

Leadership
19, 21, 66, 70, 71, 96, 115, 116, 119, 120, 132, 135, 146, 148, 166, 192, 198, 272, 326, 333

Marketing
26, 28, 48, 72, 78, 86, 87, 88, 90, 91, 92, 93, 176, 247, 268, 280, 321, 330, 334, 339

Mindfulness
106, 136, 137, 138, 140, 141, 142, 143, 250

Motivation/Motivational
105, 109, 114, 116, 117, 120, 157, 198, 204, 210, 244, 325, 331, 333

Passion/Compassion
6, 12, 16, 32, 40, 51, 78, 79, 80, 82, 83, 84, 85, 90, 93, 96, 97, 99, 103, 105, 107, 132, 133, 135, 136, 138, 139, 140, 142, 145, 147, 149, 160, 166, 167, 168, 170, 179, 182, 187, 190, 203, 204, 223, 227, 230, 234, 254, 272, 273, 274, 280, 289, 291, 296, 297, 312, 315, 316

Purpose/Purposeful
6, 11, 12, 13, 14, 15, 16, 55, 87, 90, 110, 120, 133, 134, 136, 138, 139, 140, 145, 149, 152, 154, 161, 177, 178, 179, 180, 229, 233, 245, 253, 268, 272, 273, 275, 296, 312, 313, 314, 320, 330, 331, 332

Relationship/Relationships
14, 16, 20, 23, 31, 32, 67, 69, 94, 131, 135, 137, 139, 187, 188, 189, 190, 191, 192, 195, 234, 250, 272, 290, 297

Spirit/Spiritual/Spirituality
13, 14, 16, 75, 76, 77, 82, 91, 109, 110, 178, 180, 183, 222, 226, 229, 231, 233, 234, 239, 245, 248, 249, 250, 272, 273, 274, 275, 293, 295, 296, 304, 307, 308, 314

Success/Successful
6, 7, 16, 17, 24, 32, 36, 40, 41, 47, 50, 58, 63, 71, 75, 76, 78, 80, 82, 85, 86, 87, 90, 91, 99, 101, 102, 104, 106, 107, 109, 110, 111, 112, 114, 116, 117, 118, 120, 126, 127, 128, 130, 132, 133, 136, 138, 141, 142, 144, 152, 157, 159, 160, 173, 174, 176, 186, 187, 188, 192, 254, 266, 267, 268, 270, 271, 274, 306, 307, 312, 313, 314, 316, 322, 323, 330, 331, 333

Team/Teams
15, 66, 70, 71, 74, 96, 108, 113, 119, 123, 127, 132, 133, 144, 195, 210, 255, 266, 267, 268, 275, 329, 331, 339

Transform/Transformation
10, 36, 45, 46, 71, 102, 119, 124, 149, 151, 166, 177, 230, 231, 244, 247, 248, 257, 274, 296, 299, 301, 303, 304, 307, 310, 318, 322, 334

Vision/Visionary/Visionaries
7, 16, 47, 51, 56, 59, 67, 70, 71, 72, 82, 87, 100, 101, 124,

126, 128, 130, 131, 133, 135,
136, 138, 139, 140, 141, 142,
147, 148, 149, 150, 151, 152,
153, 154, 167, 169, 170, 173,
177, 178, 223, 224, 225, 229,
231, 233, 234, 236, 240, 241,
245, 253, 254, 256, 257, 258,
260, 270, 271, 272, 273, 274,
275, 276, 277, 280, 294, 297,
298, 303, 305, 309, 313, 314,
318, 320, 326, 327, 330, 333,
334

Voyage
6, 7, 109, 119, 123, 124, 158,
241, 299, 305, 309, 320, 327

About Expert Insights Publishing

Our mission is to give authors a voice and a platform on which to stand. We specialize in books covering innovative ways to meet the personal and business challenges of the 21st century.

Through our signature, inexpensive publishing and marketing services, we help authors publish and promote their works more effectively and connect to readers in a uniquely efficient system.

We employ an experienced team of online marketing strategists, ad copywriters, graphic artists, and Web designers whose combined talents ensure beautiful books, effective online marketing campaigns at easily affordable rates, and personal attention to you and your needs.

**We have promoted over 450 authors to bestseller status.
Will you be next?**

Learn more about our current publishing opportunities at:

ExpertInsightsPublishing.com

www.ingramcontent.com/pod-product-compliance
Lightning Source LLC
Chambersburg PA
CBHW070735170426
43200CB00007B/534